ARTIFICIAL INTELLIGENCE *and* THE NEW MESSIAH

IT WAS FORETOLD – ARE WE LISTENING?

ANTHONY GARCIA

Copyright © 2021 by Anthony Garcia.

All rights reserved. No part of this publication may be reproduced, distributed or transmitted in any form or by any means, including photocopying, recording, or other electronic or mechanical methods, without the prior written permission of the publisher, except in the case of brief quotations embodied in critical reviews and certain other noncommercial uses permitted by copyright law.

Anthony Garcia/Artificial Intelligence and The New Messiah
Printed in the United States of America
www.ArtificialIntelligenceandNewMessiah.com

Although every precaution has been taken to verify the accuracy of the information contained herein, the author and publisher assume no responsibility for any errors or omissions. No liability is assumed for damages that may result from the use of information contained within.

Artificial Intelligence and The New Messiah/Anthony Garcia -- 1st ed.

ISBN 978-0-9903739-6-4 Print Edition

ISBN 978-0-9903739-8-8 Ebook Edition

Library of Congress Control Number: 2020908115

OTHER BOOKS AND SITES BY ANTHONY GARCIA

Alabados	www.Alabados.com
The Portal of Light	www.ThePortalLight.com
Shared Lives, Twin Sun	www.SharedLivesTwinSun.com
Watili, the Native American Slave Heroine	www.Watili.com
The Word Decoder	www.WordDecoder.com
Artificial Intelligence and The New Messiah	www.ArtificialIntelligenceandNewMessiah.com

THEATRE AND PLAYS

Hidden In Plain Sight	Based on novel *Edict of Faith of the Portal of Light*
Watili, the Native American Slave Heroine	Based on novel *Watili, the Native American Slave Heroine*

Contents

Proem ix

Introduction: The Discovery at Qumran xiii

1. What are the Dead Sea Scrolls? 1

2. The Essene Community and Scrolls 9

3. Historian Flavius Josephus the Essene 33

4. Who were the Original Esoteric Essenes 43

5. Messianic Conception: Role of Women at the Beginning of New Age of Aquarius 51

6. Artificial Intelligence 67

7. Who will be Messiah in Age of Aquarius and The Continuum 85

8. How will Messiah challenge powerful AI and its Human Supporters 99

9. Sephardic-Ladino Writers of Exodus Play 115

10. Esoteric Wisdom not Shared in Scrolls nor Exodus Play 123

11. The New Messiah Ushers in Catastrophic event similar to Noah 145

12. What the Future Holds with the New Messiah 153

13. The New Mother Mary will Precipitate the Arrival of the Portal of Light 169

Conclusion 175

Author's Note and Background 191

Afterword 197

Addendum A The Future Shared in the Technology of the Portal of Light 199

Appendix A How Play Characters relate to Essene History 205

Appendix B Themes Comparative Analysis Dead Sea Scrolls and Exodus Play.. 211

Glossary of Words, Phrases and Concepts 227

Bibliography 233

This book is dedicated to the following deserving communities:

The Ladino Hermanos Penitentes whom unselfishly preserved the Law of Moses in the writing of the Exodus Play and the one singular petition, How is She to be Treated?

The brotherhood concealed the prose in sacrifice of their faith and survival upon their arrival in the American Southwest.

The Judaic community of the world that has awaited their Anointed One to arrive pre-ordained by their message of a True Israel and request by the Essene Brotherhood.

A Mis Hijos, EBG, ASG, ABG and ESG

Proem

The arrival of the recent Pandemic has incited Humankind to question and reevaluate the innate moral values that have provided for an unhealthy environment to exist to permit a deadly virus to spread across the globe. The timing is consistent with the arrival of a Being of equal magnitude, the arrival in this Time Frame that has been foretold as the New Messiah. The simultaneous advent of the COVID-19 virus and the forthcoming arrival of the New Messiah is not a chance event. Rather the appearance of Pandemic death events is the sign of forerunner events that will shape the mind and expectation of the young Messiah as he or she prepares into the leadership role for society.

A significant discovery transpires on rare occasions, the light that appears caused the revealer fists to fly into the air in pure joy, history was revealing the primal origin of the sacred writers.

In the year of 2011, the Exodus play written after 1733 revealed these words.

———

How will she be treated?

———

This timepoint of this disclosure is historical, the end of times recognized by the star studious Mayans and Aztecs of 2012 and the beginning of the new age of Aquarius by the equally academic Essenes. It was within these writings that the ancient Ladino writers of the Exodus Play realized the application of Sacred Terms of the Portals, Dreams-Visions, Angels, Arithmetic Clues to the Universe, and Esoteric matters that would connect to the writings of Enoch.

A time period of the Age of Pisces was reflective of the first writes of the Judaic mystics in the books of works, known as the Words of Righteousness. The vast understanding of the Cosmos in the Bronze scrolls by Aramaic speaking Essenes provided insight into the expected significance and reason the Messiah known as Jesus of Nazareth would arrive to give hope and the historic faith to combat the Roman-Kitta.

The Essenes laid the groundwork for the understanding of forthcoming events in the Age of Aquarius and the formation of both the Corporate Elite and Artificial Intelligence. These formations will foretell the arrival of the new Messiah and Human's fate in the 21st and 22nd centuries.

This new Messiah will be known as the Anointed One by the Jewish community, reflecting the direct linkage to their faith and philosophy. The interconnection of the Judeo-Christian relationship, known as the Continuum, will be of the highest priority to this new leader. The Anointed One will realize that the Corporate Elite goal will be to remove Human conscious thinking and control society via the use of Artificial Intelligence. Forthcoming will be the battle of Believers vs. the Non-Believers, just as the Essenes had studied and written in their historic scrolls.

Telling of a future manifestation, regardless of its purpose, many times is not a welcome event. Grand life events possess their own timing and reason for their timely appearance, irrespective of your current social and political status; these life events are entirely out of one's control, the advent of a specific historical figure in the Age of Aquarius and the coming of the Anointed One.

Introduction

The Discovery at Qumran

The accidental discovery of the scrolls in Qumran in 1947, the Essene fortress residence of Masada, revealed original never known biblical writings by the Essenes that were not part of the Hebrew written Torah. The Aramaic written Book of Enoch, found among the Book of Giants, provided an exact esoteric source of reference that prior had attributed to mysterious Jewish or early mystics. The wisdom shared in these writings, provided the clarity of the usage of messenger-angels, arithmetic-coding, openings-portals, and leadership as instruments to instruct profound lessons of learning.

This history combines three primary prose, the historic Portal of Light, Kabbalah influenced Shared Light, Twin Sun both by author Anthony Garcia and The Complete Dead Sea Scrolls by Geza Vermes to provide the beginning of the Christian faith, the sharing of esoteric teachings of the original mystical Jews and the final linkage by the Essenes of our Judaic origination.

What will enlighten the reader is the disclosure and purpose of the Essenes:

ANTHONY GARCIA

Conceal the origination and history of the Judaic-Christian founding
The birthplace and family knowledge of One Jesus of Nazareth

Upon the onset of the Roman-Kitta army surrounding of Masada fortress in the year 1 BC, the Essenes committed the unthinkable in full view for the Roman empire. The entire Son of Light fraternity committed self-slaughter before the siege, providing astonishment to the invading Romans as they located slain bodies in all parts of the fort Masada. Yet the Essene self-sacrifice provided fulfillment to their engagement, to preserve the past and future of the enlightenment of the Sons of Light.

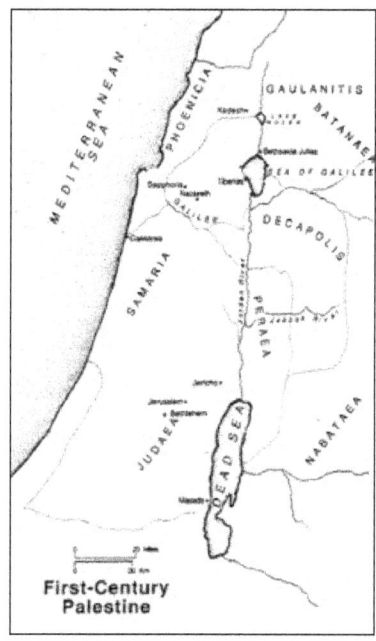

First-Century Palestine

The Essenes and the Purpose to Write and Maintain the Detailed Scrolls

The purpose of the Essene existence and finale was to conceal the family wisdom and history of the One known as the Healer. The Essenes awaited and were aware that a special one was to be earth-born at the onset of the age of Pisces, the birth time of One Jesus of Nazareth.

Extending the continued wisdom of the Essenes, known as the Continuum, a special one will be earth-born at the beginning of the age of Aquarius. Yet this new special one will be of a separate set of skills to combat the challenges of the 21st and 22nd centuries.

The Essene Sons of Light

The Essenes referred to themselves as the Sons of Light, those members that possessed the ability to comprehend and write of the cosmic clues in the sacred writings, were held in extraordinary esteem among the brotherhood.

This meant the clues of the universe were maintained in the books of esoteric knowledge, the books of Astronomy included:

> Book 1   The Watchers
> Book 2   The Parables
> Book 3   The Astronomy
> Book 4   The Dreamers
> Book 5   The Epistle of Enoch
> Book of Daniel (not in Book of Astronomy)

The Book of Enoch

The writings of Enoch are pertinent to this nonfiction novel, what makes these prose unique is the unmasking of how the characters are clarified and revealed for their purpose. The Essene authors make use of the auto antonym-dual meaning of eloquence, the use of animals to represent human beings and human beings to represent angels.

The Book of Enoch was a religious text ascribed by tradition to Enoch, the great-grandfather of Noah. The writings of the book contain material of the origins of demons, giants, watchers, angels and an explanation of how the Genesis flood was necessary.

Interpreting the Secret Cosmic Knowledge of the Essene Matter

Interpreting the Scrolls' cryptic writings of the original books is of great importance to humankind. Much of the esoteric cosmic knowledge of the Essenes has not been discovered within the caves of Qumran, and this implies whatever knowledge possessed by the Essenes has not been located. Much of the cosmic wisdom was placed on the Bronze scrolls. The discovery of the stories of how the Essene sacred scholars gathered and inscribed their cryptic knowledge upon the scrolls is as important as is the discovery of the scrolls themselves. This insight may disclose the source of the original thoughts and motivations to conceal such influential matter within the scrolls themselves.

The Sephardim have learned that the real value of cloaking wisdom is comprehending the thoughts and motivations of those concealing the matter in any form. This matter, albeit in cosmic knowledge, philosophy, hidden values of the sacred writers, is what lives forward for another day to be shared.

To make sense of organic Essene wisdom is the ability to pass orally forward to future generations the knowledge of how to use the spirit of the angel Uriel, this acquisition of esoteric matter will be of great importance to the New Messiah.

Discovery of Similar Souls of Knowledge: The Continuum

It is with the Discovery of similar souls of knowledge and concealment that join the two brotherhoods, the Sons of Light-Essenes and Brothers of Light-Ladino Hermanos from the Portal of Light prose, of the absolute faith to survive millennia without sacrificing or diluting the true inner historical belief of the value of the Essenes.

This evolution of knowledge and lessons learned will forever create the interdependent concept known as the Continuum, the new leader, and the Anointed One will recognize the Judeo Christian bond that will provide the basis of leadership into the 21st and 22nd century.

Passing orally forward to future generations, the knowledge of how to use the spirit of the angel Uriel, this wisdom captured in the Essenes Book of Astrology.

Today's Space Satellite Validation in The Age of Aquarius

In the 21st century, satellite technology permits the validation of the Essene arithmetic analysis into the cosmos.

In November of 2003, the Hubble Space Telescope located the First Sun-Semano in the Dabih Major constellation of Capricorneus, publishing this find in November of 2014, known as galaxy cluster MS2137.3-2553.

The Semano is a burned-out blue-white star, was 8 billion years older and four times as big as our current Sun. It is known as a planetary nebula or white dwarf star that gave life to the planets in our Milky Way. Since part of the same galaxy, they are known as sister stars or a double Sun within the same galaxy.

Why the sister stars were selected as the original heavens for the Ladino Hermanos is a mystery. One possibility is they selected the Dabih Major galaxy that possessed a star system where a young newborn star could be manipulated into a Portal of Light. What is certain is that the clues to locate the constellation Capricorneus were left to be discovered. This provides insight as to the hidden values of these original sacred writers.

Theme Comparative Analysis (Appendix B)

The Comparative Analysis provides the extrasensory depth of understanding of the past present and future relationship between the historic Essenes and the present-day Ladino communities. The shared philosophical and esoteric correlation of the minds to apply the concepts of the Continuum and the anticipation of the New Messiah is shared in these pages, this providing the portal of shared knowledge of the forthcoming events to take place.

Request by The Ladino Hermanos

The Ladino Hermanos that originate from the lonely Moradas of northern New Mexico and southern Colorado genuinely requested the arrival of what they entitled the new Messiah or Emmanuel. Upon the acknowledgement and answer of this long-term passive prayer perdition, the Creator-Higher God will provide the Anointed One at the entrance into the age of Aquarius at the bequest of this repressed Jewish community.

This genuine enlightenment will unselfishly provide solutions to the many issues and problems of today, just as the Creator has designed. As always, it will not arrive without sacrifice, just as the Ladino community has sacrificed for hundreds of years.

The sacrifice by the Ladino Hermanos has been lengthy, some punished, embarrassed, and led to slaughter by the Inquisitors, many hidden in plain sight, others living dual faith lives. Survival of a person and their faith is funny, there is no logic to describe it or reason to justify its strange actions to outsiders.

I am often asked why does not this community or person's just open up and disclose themselves in this free society of today? The answer is survival; to conceal oneself is survival just as the Essenes concealed of their wisdom and knowledge of the new significant earthborn.

Anthony Garcia

1

What are The Dead Sea Scrolls

The discovery of the first Dead Sea Scrolls in a remote Judean Desert cave in 1947 is widely considered the most significant archaeological event of the twentieth century. Bedouin treasure hunters and archaeologists ultimately found the remains of hundreds of ancient scrolls. These fragile pieces of parchment and papyrus, including the oldest existing copies of the Hebrew Bible, were preserved for two thousand years by the hot, desert climate and the darkness of the caves where they were placed. The scrolls provide an unprecedented picture of the diverse religious beliefs of ancient Judaism, and daily life during the turbulent Second Temple period.

The scrolls themselves are written upon parchment animal skin and papyrus, they were written mostly in Hebrew but also Greek and the Aramaic. The longest scroll (written in Hebrew) measured up to twenty-seven feet in length.

Of the 930 scrolls located in Qumran, they were separated into the following categories:

230 or 25% copies of Hebrew Bible (except Esther and Ezra)
250 or 27% Common Judaism
350 or 38% Sectarian –Theology, Beliefs, Practices
100 or 10% Either Sectarian or Non-Sectaran of Qumran sect itself

Example of Important Scrolls Already Included in Torah-Tenash

Genesis: the oldest known copies ever of Genesis, the scrolls contain the description of the first three days of the creation of the world.

The Ten Commandments: This scroll maintains one of the earliest known copies of the Ten Commandments, a central doctrine in Judaism and Christianity.

Psalms: This book is one of the best-preserved scrolls containing 48 psalms, including seven new psalms that are not found in standard Masoretic version written by King David.

Twelve Minor Profits: Assemblage of sort prophetic books into a single literary work. This a Greek translation of Minor Prophets maintains a prophecy of Micah about the End of Days and the rise of a ruler out of Bethlehem.

The Book of Lamech: Also called the Scroll of the Apocryphal Genesis. Written in Aramaic, this scroll seems to be the Book of Genesis. It describes the journeys of Abraham, the beauty of Sarah, his wife, and a recount of Noah's birth. This scroll was so deteriorated, it was seven years before it could be unrolled.

Daniel: The Aramaic Apocryphon of Daniel describes either a messianic figure or a boastful ruler that will arise as "Son of God" or "Son of the Most High" as a redeemer.

The Scrolls provided emphasis on sacred works included in the Torah and never seen before works that broadened the understanding of faith. It is for this reason, the scrolls are essential for different reasons for unique faiths.

What Scrolls or Books Were Located in Qumran That Were Not Part of Torah-Tenash

Book of Enoch: The book of Enoch was not included in the Hebrew Bible. Enoch, the great-grandson of Noah who lived 365 years and "walked with God" is singularly recognized in Genesis.

Book of Esther: Relates the story of a Hebrew woman in Persia born as Hadassah but known as Esther, that becomes queen of Persia and thwarts a genocide of her community and later becomes the core of festival of Purim.

Book of Ezra/Nehemiah: Tells of successive missions to Jerusalem by Ezra and Nehemiah and their efforts to restore the worship of the God of Israel and to create a purified community.

Community Rule of Essene origin: These scrolls maintains laws and rules meant for members of the Essene community. The scrolls provide insight into the religious and social lives of this group that survives their structure of leadership of hierarchical priestly society.

Rule of Blessings: Includes three benedictions for the use during eschaton-end of times.

Copper Scrolls: likely provides fictitious locations of hidden gold and silver caves, the real treasure is the Aramaic description of Zodiac calendar that demonstrates Essene knowledge of Constellations and importance of Celestial Equator.

Copper Scrolls were Essene in origin and written in Aramaic, preserving the Zodiac Calendar share knowledge of Constellation movement and the celestial equator, they were of great importance to Judaic mystics. Several of the scrolls housed 'horoscopes' or, more precisely, documents of astrological physiognomy, a literary genre based on the belief that the temper, physical features, and fate of an individual depend on the configuration of the heavens at the time of the person's birth.

> *Copper Scrolls were Essene in origin and written in Aramaic, preserving the Zodiac Calendar*

Book of War of Essene origin: Details an apocalyptic 40-year old battle between the forces of good and evil. These fragments share a blessing to be recited by the leader of the surviving community upon their victory in the final battle at the end of time.

Why Scrolls are Important to Different Faiths:
Jewish:

The discovery of the Dead Sea Scrolls represents a turning point in the study of the history of the Jewish people in ancient times, for never before has a literary treasure of such magnitude come to light. Thanks to these remarkable discoveries, knowledge of Jewish and Essene societies in Judea during the Hellenistic and Roman periods, as well as the origins of rabbinical Judaism and early Christianity, has been greatly enriched.

For the Jewish community, this is emotional, and a treasure found directly from this scroll by their forefathers 2,000 years ago.

Some texts that are slightly different, usually just in the spelling of a word here or there, yet other books are entirely intact. Until the Scrolls were discovered, the books of Flavius Josephus and the books of Maccabees provided the main source of historical insight into this period. Prior to the scroll discovery, the oldest complete Hebrew Bible was the Leningrad Codex (a.d. 1008).

Christians:

The scrolls illuminate the understanding of the early Christians. None of the Qumran scrolls was written by or for Christians. Three books most commonly found at Qumran are Psalms (36 scrolls), Deuteronomy (30), and Isaiah (21). This is hardly a coincidence but speaks to similar messianic expectations and covenantal themes among the Essenes and the early Christians.

The most essential enlightenment for Christians is the scrolls demonstrated the life portrayed by John the Baptist, as a wilderness preacher that eschewed the living values of the Essene community.

This exhibits the upbringing and training of knowledge of one Jesus of Nazareth, who later was proclaimed the Messiah by his immediate family and other followers of his preaching.

The Messianic Apocalypse and New Testament

The Essene written Messianic Apocalypse (4Q521) is referred to as the 'Resurrection Fragment', the ability of the forthcoming Messiah, this writing consists of sixteen fragments dated to the beginning of the first century BC. Written approximately 150 years before Luke's Gospel (7, 21-22), it shares an interpretive and theological tradition that both the Essenes and the early Christians drew. Common words are the following:

BIBLE	ESSENES
<u>Luke</u>	<u>4Q521</u>
Cured Many	Cured Many
Blind See	Blind See
Dead Raised	Dead Raised
Good News to Poor	Good News to Poor

This comparative demonstrates the origin of the Messiah expected by both communities and discloses the connection between the two groups. These two distinct and separate groups drew from their expectation of the Messiah of the origin as a healer.

Islam

The Koran maintains some of the principal history of the Torah, most specifically the first five books of the Hebrew Bible and the recognizable figures such as Abraham, Moses, Lot, Noah, Tubal, and others. The scrolls are of importance to Islam, for they maintain the earliest known shared segments of both Judaic and Islam history.

The shared interrelationship provides a common platform of education and teaching, specific members of the Essene community were sent into exile after a division occurred within the Essene brotherhood and a large encampment were sent into the *Lands Further North* of Damascus, Syria; *exiling the Tabernacle of the King and resurrecting the Fallen Tent of David* (Amos 5:26–27 and 9:11), may place this exiled community in northern lands influencing both philosophy and sharing the of faith of religious education directly from the Essene community.

This exile likely occurred after the *Period of Wrath*, which followed the destruction by Nebuchadnezzar (ascended to the throne of Babylon in 605 BC). Still, later God *raised a bud who became Teach of Righteousness-Interpreter of the Law*, who *went out of the Land of Judah*. This may place the exile to the northern Middle East communities and beyond likely in 400+ BC.

In our modern time frame, Qumran was under British and later Jordanian rule at the time of the discoveries was taken over by Israel after the 1967 war and is now being challenged by Jordan. Palestinian National Authority and the Jordanian government contesting Israel's claim to ownership of the scrolls, The Israel government is not discussing the return scrolls back to either party.

Tunnel from Jerusalem

In September 2007, a tunnel leading from Jerusalem to the area of Qumran was found, suggesting that some of the scrolls and other treasures from the Temple were brought to the area to hide from the Roman destruction.

Also, in September 2017, a 14th cave may have been located with shards of pottery, and scroll remains. Continuing the speculation of new caves in the Qumran exist.

2

The Essene Community and Scrolls

The Essene community became of importance when in 1947, the Dead Sea Scrolls were located in the Qumran caves at the desert fortress of Masada-*Matuza* near the Dead Sea of Judea, 13 miles east of Jerusalem.

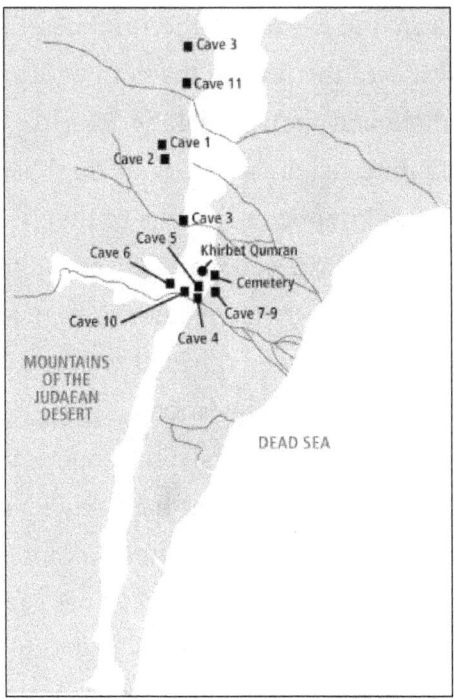

The thirteen caves housed over 930 scrolls mostly in jars, many were located with thousands of pieces of jar and scroll fragments. Most intact scrolls were wrapped in a thin cloth wrap and the leather strap that bound the scrolls the jars once held.

The scrolls enhanced our knowledge of both Judaism and Christianity and are considered the evolutionary link between the two. Hidden and preserved in jars hidden in caves that dated back to the siege of Jerusalem by the Roman-Kitta.

It was soon determined that the scrolls were hidden within the auspices of an unlikely community group with roots to the ancient Judaic writings and philosophy of the original pioneers of Judaic text and faith. This obscure and mysterious Torah believing sect were called the Essenes, meaning the Community. The Essenes lived within an equality-based community philosophy that eschewed materialism and existed in the rural deserts of Palestine. The Essenes considered themselves the faith of *True Israel*, as opposed to the temple and money-making Pharisee communities. The established ruling religious orders of the Pharisees did not view the religious philosophy or lifestyle of the Essenes as an acceptable way of life that eschewed materialism and thus kept a distance from this religious sect. The Pharisees were aware that this group maintained an unmatched spiritual zeal, and their loyalty to the Torah writings was without question.

With this separation of spiritual philosophy, and unpopular views towards each other, why would the likely Pharisees elect to hide their most prized religious texts among a community that eschewed their existence? Members of the Essenes gave up all material goods and assets to the collective of the brotherhood to become members. Essenes considered themselves vastly more spiritual in connection to God than the Pharisees and adhered to the concept Oneness of the Creature and Nature.

The scrolls were hidden in the caves around A.D. 68, just before the destruction of the Second Temple in 70 A.D., The Pharisees surmised the Romans would come upon the Temple in Jerusalem and not locate the Holy scriptures and begin torturing Temple priests and members to disclose the location of the scrolls. The Temple priest elders recognized that for their scrolls to survive, devotion to their faith and an uncharacteristic source to conceal the scrolls was the only chance of survival of their written history, their unnatural selection, the Essenes fortress in Masada The Pharisee priests presumed that the Romans would discover this unorthodox faithful sect but not infer that the Holy documents not located in the Temple would be concealed within their fortress. The Essenes nature bound style of spirituality would provide the camouflage of a society that would not partake in a revolt and be incapable of waging war to threaten the Romans.

The Essene community provided a deceptive nature living a lifestyle that extolled a masquerade that they possessed any knowledge of the sacred scrolls of the Pharisees but yet were devout followers of the law of the Torah. This camouflage provided the distractions for the Romans not to think the Essenes knew of the whereabouts of the Holy scripture. Essene elders requested that specific members dig deep into the cavers near and far from the fortress, to conceal and confuse the Roman-Kitta from locating their treasures. Other Essene members volunteered to excavate caves at night and not divulge the location of the caves. Those caves closest to the fortress would house the Essene library, and those furthest from the fortress, would hide the Pharisee scrolls and items. Throughout time, nature, water and earthquakes, eventually covered the openings of these caves until the *Ta'amireh* Bedouin shepherds accidentally uncovered one cave in the year 1947.

Who Were the Essenes:
How They Lived:

The Essenes were a community of mostly celibate men and a few families that walked away for city life and formal religious practices of the Temple (Although most considered themselves still Pharisees) for a life that provided a deeper relationship with the Creator, the Higher-Being God and an Oneness with nature and spiritual, and considered themselves True Israel. They lived in seclusion, and recruits all came from outside the society. They were two separate types of groups, the desert sect that lived in the rural deserts of Palestine, and the group that lived in the fortress in Masada with 13 cisterns for bathing, and their unique lifestyle stood separate from the every-day lifestyle of most Palestinians.

The Essene city sect was grouped in families and were not the celebrant. The property was owned individually, and all men were ordered to pay two days wages every month to a charitable fund to assist in paying those unable to pay, other members that possessed health conditions, and women that were widowed.

Both groups led by *Zodikite* priestly family, yet operational decisions were governed by *Megaqqer* or the Guardians of the society. The Guardians applied the Community rules in matters of doctrine, discipline, purity, impurity and everything relating to *justice and property.* All members embraced the solar calendar and liturgical Law of Moses texts.

The word Essene means Community and this group called themselves Judah-*Yahad*. They flourished during the Second Temple era. (c. 250 BC– 70 CE) with a stronghold in rural regions such as Galilee near the Sea of Galilee. The Essenes possessed a fervent connection to the land, voided use of Iron Age objects such as jewelry or combs.

Despise of riches there is no one to be found who hath more than another, those who come to live with them granted their possession to be common to the whole order. There was no appearance of poverty or excess riches and everyone's personal possession are intermingled with others, only one patrimony. Yet each member had a steward appointed to take of their common affairs such as obtaining specific plants and seeds for medicinal healing.

Ritual immersion in water from a living water source—established as a practice in the book of Leviticus—was understood to render the Jew ritually clean, enabling him or her to enter certain pure or sacred areas. Bathing twice a day in almost frigid cold water was a normal occurrence before meals or prayer rituals. Men wore white loin-cloth briefs and women simple white dresses, bathing before one-course meals were served. The use of incense was prohibited and the dependency upon bathing was of significant importance to provide cleansing to the order. With 13 cisterns for bathing in Masada, this was a very important ritual practiced at this time. To become a member of the Essenes, initial immersion was the first act in a lifelong practice of ritual immersion.

Essenes were a healing community, living in a region where blindness, leprosy, bent back and injury of some sort was of the common place, the Essenes saw themselves and practiced the art of ritual healing. The use of medicinal plants and prayer was used to the curing of the blind, the straightening of the bent, the healing of the wounded, the raising of the dead, and the proclamation of the *Good News* to the poor. Ritual practices for Purification of eating or bathing, renewal of covenants, Confession, Marriage, Battle, adhered to a set of Community rules bound to the rituals.

They are very careful not to exhibit their anger, carefully controlling such outbursts. They are very loyal and are peacemakers. They refuse to swear oaths, believing every word they speak to be stronger than an oath. They are scrupulous students of the ancient literature. They are ardent students in the healing of diseases, of the roots offering protection, and of the properties of stones.
Flavius Josephus, War 2

As strict Torah observant, messianic, apocalyptic, Baptist yielding, wilderness living, and new covenant Jewish believers, they considered themselves "Sons of Light", or the "Poor," members of "the way" and "holy ones" who lived in the "house of holiness" for the "Holy Spirit" lived within them. They were led by the "Teacher of Righteousness," though was never identified this person in the scrolls.

They also took great pains in studying the writings of the ancients and choose out of them what is most for the advantage of their soul and body. Study of the books of Ezekiel, Isaiah, Psalms, along with Genesis, Exodus, Deuteronomy and Numbers writings, was common.

The Qumran sectary had more particularly to perform the ritual acts prescribed by Moses in the correct manner and at the right times. The earthly liturgy was intended to be a replica of that sung by the choirs of angels in the celestial Temple.

There were no separate businesses permitted for members. They could not either buy or sell anything to one another and yet were fully allowed to take what they want of whosoever they withed. They rejected personal pleasures as an evil, but esteem continence or celibacy, and the conquest over our passions, to be a virtue. They neglected wedlock but did not deny the fitness of marriage and the succession of mankind.

They ate as a group twice daily and clothed themselves in white veils before bathing in cold water before entering the dining room for meals, saying grace before and after meals.

They did not allow for the change of daily garments, or of shoes, till they are first entirely torn to pieces or worn out by time. They carry nothing with them when they travel to remote parts and search for new Essene communities with which to lay their head and reside for a time.

They held residential property in nearly all of the big cities and in Jerusalem. They traveled with the clothes on their backs to other small towns or cities, citing the *Good News* or as part of a Disciples led group. Often living off nature in their travels and connecting with the Oneness of nature and God. They believed One must find that place of balance at the very core of their being. This is where one will find one's true Self, where One will find God, where One will find Peace and Joy. This spiritual connection with nature is not found in today's New Testament.

The Essene community welcomed philosophers, musicians, healers from all parts to share of their knowledge of their specialty. One did not have to travel to India to encounter music and teachings of eastern influence. The open and broad-minded curiosity of the Essenes only added depth to their worldly point of view of life itself.

Interestingly, this important spiritual society was never mentioned in the New Testament nor the Torah.

John the Baptist, The Essene

John the Baptist was born to advanced age parents of the New Testament mother Elizabeth and his father Zechariah a temple trained priest around year 30 B.C. Elizabeth was the first cousin to Mary, mother of Jesus of Nazareth. This family raised in the Holy Mount Carmel area of Northern Israel in the Galilee region, which was home to the mystic prophet sect called the Essenes.

Growing up in Galilee, John lost both his parents and was likely raised as an Essene along with his grandmother Anne and Grandfather Joachim, both prominent society members of that region.

As a young man, John lived in the wilderness or lived off of the land as the Essenes felt they were close to God in the solitude desert-like ambiance and eschewed the organized temple religion of the Pharisees.

As a young man, John began to preach in the rural lands and became known to baptism in water, which was not a normal protocol for Essenes. His message was controversial and turned off many a Pharisee. A point of view influenced from his knowledge as an Essene philosophy, that you were placing your faith in the future messiah, not in the temple system. He wore clothes of camels' hair and only ate locusts and honey; this logically made sense if John took the Qumran vow of not eating foods or wearing clothing outside of the Community Rule of Living.

John attracted his own disciples and became known as John the Baptists for the eloquent sayings of providing ritual cleaning of purification in the waters of the Galilee sea as he baptized young and old alike, practice was not consistent with Essenes teachings. John required that each time an adherent would be immersed, he must first reflect upon the condition of his heart and repent if necessary. The confession of sin and unworthiness played an important role in exhibiting one's readiness for membership.

Freely sharing his vision of the future of a new Messiah and drawing crowds, he came to baptize as a ritual of the spiritually unclean as submerged many from near and far alike. John had a more liberal view of the tenets of his Essene brotherhood, preferring to embrace all differences, yet still, remain connected to the brotherhood teachings and philosophy.

Away from trained priests and formal temples, John freely evoked his views upon new Judea ruled Roman commanders that ruled Judea and their non-traditional lifestyles and idolatry practices. This drew the attention of one Roman soldier that incarcerated him and admonished him publicly.

There John sat in a Roman jail, awaiting his fate from the Roman king of Galilee.

In jail, others began to ask him about Jesus and they all began to talk of healing and preaching capabilities of one Jesus of Nazareth. Then John asked one of his disciples to go and ask Jesus this question. *Are you the one who is to come, or should we expect someone else?*

Jesus of Nazareth replied, "Go back and report to John what you hear and see, The blind receive sight, the lame walk, the lepers are cleansed, the deaf hear, the dead are raised, and good news is preached to the poor....
(Mathew 11:5)

The answer provided by the Nazarene was that he provided community value in his life as if trained and lived as an Essene. Healing and prayer were the virtues of an Essene and this is how Jesus lived likely as a young man and when he began preaching the *Good News*.

What the Essenes Believed in The Arrival Point of The Romans

The use of the concept of Son of Light to fulfill the testament of good health was used as a technique to work and share work in the community and the link between the Creator and humankind. They valued Oneness of Nature and Spirituality as their demonstrative of genuine faith, similar to ethnic native indigenous cultures in other parts of the world.

The believed in Voluntary poverty and collective ownership while serving each other, this considerably different from the organized Pharisee religion of Judea.

Abstained from anointing themselves with oils, a practice common among Pharisees, living in an arid climate, they preferred to live in a state of sweat and then bathed daily-*mikvah*. The bathing pools placed one set of stairs exist for you to use on your way in, and another on your way out, that way your "clean" feet don't touch where your unclean feet once trotted. This was permitted by the Masada aqueducts that were built that diverted water from distant underground pools into large cisterns within the fortress.

The Pharisees represented a group of lay teachers of the Torah. The Pharisees were linked to the urban middle classes and took their name from their life of separation from ritual impurity and untithed produce. (The Sadduces lay group in 1st-century b.c. had not formed) The Community desired to live as One with nature and sought out medicinal roots for remedies of healing the body and soul. Fires were used to warm hot stones to remedy ailments such as arthritis or to restore body balance with nature. The Judah forbid swearing in any form and spent much time discussing religious and spiritual philosophy.

The Essenes considered themselves the guardians of the Divine Teaching. They had in their possession a significant number of very ancient manuscripts, some of them going back to the dawn of time. A large portion of the school members spent their time decoding them, translating them into several languages, and reproducing them, to perpetuate and preserve this advanced knowledge. They considered this work to be a sacred task.

The study of the ancient writers of the books of Enoch, Daniel, Ezekiel, Tobit, Noah, and Moses was the common practice. The Essenes created their own rules of life writings pertaining to the books of the Community, Meditation, War. This framework followed a very disciplined and regimented lifestyle.

When the Essenes felt repressed, or as a societal group that is threatened, they called upon a child-born Messiah to provide freedom from their oppressor, the Roman-Kitta or even the Pharisees. The Essenes used the War Scrolls and writings using Michael (Melchizedek) as the "Prince of Light" against their foe the Devil (Belial) "The Son of Darkness" foreknown as the polytheism believing Roman-Kitta.

At the time of the hiding of the scrolls, the Essenes were expecting an end of times cataclysmic event that coincided with the end of Aries ended and the beginning of the age of Pisces. This event may have been the upcoming invasion by the Romans and their violent history of sieges and the burning of religious entities and historical texts. The elders were aware that the Romans eastern campaign conquered the provinces of Pompey, Alexandria and Syria before placing their sights upon Palestine and Jerusalem.

Esoteric Knowledge

The initial esoteric-Judaic mysticism study and analysis of the cosmos originated within the Essene community in and around Palestine. One of the first concepts learned by Essenes was the passage of the time, use of the Solar Calendar year. A tropical year that is divided into 24 solar terms, a separate 15 segments of solar longitude to assist in tracing the celestial equilibrium. The time required for the Earth to rotate around the Sun is one solar year. The solar calendar typically measures the time between vernal equinoxes.

To a young Jesus of Nazareth, Passover meant more than just a Seder meal. When the sun passes over (Passover), the celestial equator heading up to the Tropic of Cancer, it provides us with the clarity of the spring and summer months, days are longer than nights. This the preferred time to plant and care for large gardens that the Essene were dependent upon for their survival.

Those members especially affiliated with the wisdom of the Aramaic language, were prone to maintain this insight, this spoken in and around Galilee. The Cosmic insight and study of the constellations belonged to this select group originated in rural desert, especially among sheepherders, although this ingenuity was never shared within the scrolls. The important Copper Scrolls containing the Zodiac Calendar were partially written in Aramaic, those found in Cave 3. (Copper Scroll 3Q15)

The continued study of the cosmos and constellation is necessary to grasp the constant movement of star patterns, equators in relation to the sun. The north celestial pole shifts as the centuries go by, the gradual change in the direction of the earth's axis in space or as the earth's axis wobbles (called precession), and as a consequence describes a circle in the sky will adjust. At the Polaris at the time of the first century, the north star was the bright Guardian *Kochab*. Today, the Polaris North star is located in the constellation *Ursa Minor*, the star is called *Stella Polaris*.

This Essene group prayed and requested for an earth-born child Messiah arrival to counter the expected cataclysmic event such as the arrival of the Romans, coinciding with the transfer of ages of Aries to Pisces. The expectation was that the Messiah could galvanize Judea to fight and impede the Roman siege upon Judea. This was distinctive from the Pharisees that requested a combat-ready adult-Messiah from heaven to lead and galvanize Judaea against the Romans.

The Arrival of New Age

Early in the first century, the Essene acknowledgment of the shifting of the constellation of Aries and into the entrance of the constellation of Pisces age required monitoring the equinox movements. As a very slow occurrence, the movement of the equinoxes by just one degree in the sky validated the new age arrival. This observation may take a human lifetime to monitor and track. It was with this expectation that a significant biblical figure would appear at the exact timing of the arrival of the Roman-Kitta that promulgated the appearance of a new Messiah.

Philosophical Difference between Essenes and Pharisees at the inception of First Century

Ezekiel's Vision of The Chariot Ascent to Defend Judea

At an early time in Essene written history, there were two schools of thought differentiating themselves, and the tie to Ezekiel's version of the "chariot ascent' was the key to grasping the placement in time the people of Judea found themselves.

The first was the Yeridah-Markalot vision of the chariot, the "Throne has been seated in Chariot" and that if the Chariot "Appears," it can be seen.

To Praise God, one must "See the Image of the Throned Chariot," To see the seated Throne was the key to grasping the chariot as an image to recruit men or young boys to rebel and fight the Romans.

The second is *Herkhalot*; the vision of the chariot is not a vision, rather is a Palace or a place,"the ascent does of the chariot does not culminate in a vision, but rather in the *merkavah* mystic's participation in the heavenly liturgy." This was not a spiritual literacy of how one should orientate in the chariot.

The first *Markalot* version of the seated throne also fit the Pharisees philosophy of a seated throne, for they were attempting to galvanize Judaic fighters against the imminent war with the Romans and required an image of a "visual chariot" raise the spirit of fighters to fight the Romans.

These were sectarian Jews the Essenes, that sought a way that they could continue to worship God spiritually, without actually having to make sacrifices at the Temple. Although both schools of thought considered themselves to be Pharisee for the most part, they lived in the desolate desert or rural areas where Temples did not exist.

The Pharisee Decision to Hide Scrolls in Caves Near the Essene-Masada Fort

The leadership of the Pharisee Temple spent months collecting the sacred writing from all of Judea and began looking for a location that the Romans would never consider when they did not find the sacred writings they so much wanted to exterminate. The leadership thought of all groups within Judea, who would be most likely to commit and preserve the writing. It became clear to them that those who study ancient books would be most safe to preserve the works.

The studious commitment of members of the Essenes to the ancient writers of the books of Enoch, Daniel, and Ezekiel provided the level of trust sought by the Pharisee leadership. Pharisees knew their sacred scripture came in from the desolate deserts to become their law of Moses, that was long ago, yet the Essenes maintained this desolate commitment to knowledge.

While many in the band of Judah still accepted being Pharisees themselves, they may not be regular members that attended Temple on the Sabbath. The Sabbath day for the Essenes was not typically practiced at Temple in desolate rural areas, although no business and customs were practiced. This was sufficient for the Pharisees to entrust.

The Essene's were known as recluses, a non-materialistic, spiritual based community that followed a passive plant-based lifestyle that did not pose a threat to the incoming Roma-Kitta army. A mystery to the Pharisee leadership, would the brotherhood be considered loyal to the dominant group or be able to conceal the sacred writings that the Romans would be in search of and never locate.

One conclusion was evident, and the Pharisees returned to their roots of faith to gamble on the protection of their written history.

The placing of the scrolls in various caves around the fort was done prior to the invasion by the Roman army. The Pharisee anticipated this attack and selected a location and a community that posed no threat or would be considered a passive community with no relationship to the Temple or its leadership.

The Essene Decision to Hide Scrolls and the Outcome of Their Fate

The elder Essenes motivation to hide scrolls was four-part:

1. Knowledge that imminent the invasion by the Roman's was forthcoming;

2. Pharisees request to conceal the sacred writing's among the Essene fortress at Masada;

3. Essenes desire to conceal their sacred works within caves near the fortress;

4. Upon the expected arrival of the Roman army, what fate awaited the Community;

The unnamed leader of the Essenes known as the Teacher of Righteousness likely participated in the decision to conceal all sacred works in anticipation of the Roman army arrival, covert caves near and around the Masada were selected. The elder Essene council decision that the closest and better-ventilated caves near the fortress would preserve the Essene historic works, some since the beginning of time, the closely held writings and scrolls were for study. The Pharisee scrolls, pottery, coins, leather phylacteries, sandals, combs cups, and other such items were concealed in a dis-oriented and hurried fashion the caves distant from the fortress.

The Essene elders also made the decision to not place in any the caves any of the esoteric knowledge of the cosmos or detailed zodiac wisdom that the community possessed. This insight would stay with those members that studied the stars, moon and constellation movements, for this may never be discovered by the Roman-Kitta.

The Esoteric scrolls were likely kept outside of the caves within the vestiges of the Aramaic speaking members that studied and believed in the cosmos analysis. Falling into the hands of both the Pharisees and Romans was not the intent of the esoteric brotherhood of the Essenes. Eschewed historically by the Pharisees, the brothers that studied the cosmos were very apprehensive of the Pharisees wanting to hide their sacred text near Masada.

What the Essenes possessed of most importance was the Spirit of the Light obtained directly from the Creator. This sprit transcended air-born time and space carried forward to bridge the consciousness of minds forever forward. The real wisdom is the understanding is the Spirit of Light that forever passed forward to the writers of the Ladino writers of the Exodus play, no words can describe the air-born wisdom that is transferred over time.

> *What the Essenes possessed of most importance was the Spirit of the Light obtained directly from the Creator.*

Prior to the final siege by the Romans, the fort Masada leadership itself was taken over by Zealots-*Secarii*, this group was set upon rebelling and fighting against the incoming invasion by Roman-Kitta army. The imminent attack by the Roman Kitta changed the philosophical temperament of those inside the

Masada fort dramatically, survival fears within the fort was permeating thought and among the Community.

This leadership philosophy changed quickly and the Zealot group separated those men of action similar to themselves, that we're willing to battle for the history of Judea, versus men of a more peaceful and visionary nature, and not men of battle. These passive men eschewed violence in any form and some were now aware of the new philosophy of Christianity. The Zealots quickly identified those persons willing to fight against the Kitta versus those that were not willing to fight against the Kitta.

Upon arrival and establishment of the Roman army base camp at the outskirts of the Masada fortress awaiting orders to sack the stronghold, all Essenes agreed to control their fate. All members of the Community committed suicide by the sword to not disclose the existence of either their scrolls or the scrolls and items left to hide by the Pharisees. The esoteric scrolls were smuggled out of the Masada to live and tell of their unique stories in other locations of the world.

Yet little of the above was ever mentioned in the Torah Pentateuch or the Bible, but of vast importance to the existence and survival of the Essene community. The rural living Essenes discretely maintained both written and esoteric knowledge of their community and this contributed to the legend of the cosmic Judaic mystics, yet much of wisdom came from the organized community of the Essenes themselves at Masada.

Pharisee Temple Jews were not taught to study celestial equinoxes, portals, angels, vestiges of esoteric wisdom. Churches, Priests and Ministers never mention Essene or the study of the young Jesus of Nazareth. This esoteric wisdom that survived later become the primary wisdom lineage of the Aramaic written Kabbalah of 14th century Spain.

Location of Existing Caves and The Ledgers of Undiscovered Tunnels

The caves closest to the site were chiseled out by hand from the soft, marl sandstone upon which *Khirbet* Qumran was built. These caves, which were closer to the site and better ventilated, served as residences for Qumran's inhabitants. The residential Qumran caves (with the exception of Cave 4—see below) contained only a smattering of scrolls kept for private study and personal devotion. The important Copper Scroll was reserved in Cave 3 near the fortress and most likely written by the esoteric Essenes.

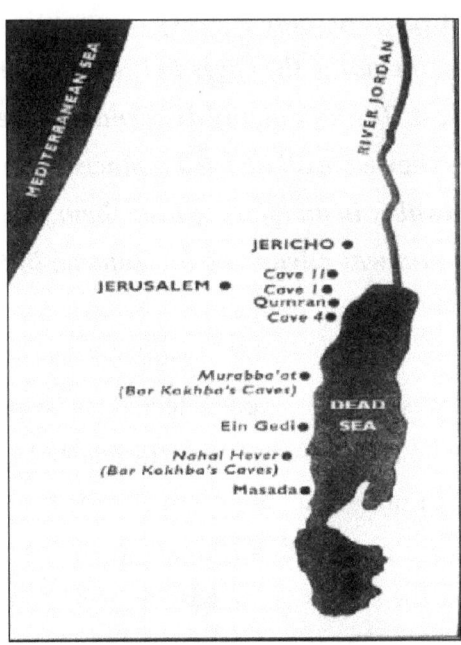

Beyond the immediate sandstone terrace, however, is another set of Qumran caves. These natural caves, which penetrate the imposing and darkened limestone cliffs above Qumran, were used to hide many of the longer and more complete Dead Sea Scrolls, including the War Scroll and the Temple Scroll. The presence of these scrolls, which often reflect a sectarian Jewish worldview. Indicates the scrolls were hidden by the local Qumran community, not by desperate Temple priests fleeing the Roman destruction of Jerusalem.

Cave 4, a residential cave in the marl terrace, however, was found littered with thousands of jumbled scroll fragments representing more than 500 separate documents written across a span of nearly three centuries. According to Biblical Archeologist Sidnie White Crawford, almost every composition found in the other ten caves, including the caves in the limestone cliffs, is also found in Cave 4. The lack of any discernable order among the texts suggests they were all hurriedly placed in the cave at the same time, possibly in an effort to hide them from the Roman legion that was advancing on Qumran in 68 C.E

Thirty seven caves or more were selected in no particular order and mapped by both Pharisee and Essene leadership, spread out at different levels to not attract attention nor far from the Dead Sea itself. Hidden with mostly identical jars in an area with hundreds of natural caves, the scrolls of the Essenes were concealed in caves closest to the Masada, due to the better ventilation in the caves the fort provided. The leadership was aware of the slaughter that Romans brought upon other cities and cultures they sieged. Thus, there was no telling the severity and length Roman rule would endure.

Clearly, a ledger of the cave location would have been created, maintained by both elder Pharisees and Essenes in order to locate the buried caves at a later date. This ledger has never been located, yet most likely, the Essenes would have buried this critical document along with other crucial deemed material to their elders in an easy to discover cavern.

Over time, earthquakes, time and nature all caused the caves to enclose and almost disappear the sacred texts from existence. Then a young Libyan Bedouin playing in the rocky drought area near Masada, threw a ball into a cave and heard the sound of broken clay pots.

3

Historian Flavius Josephus The Essene

It was to my surprise to locate two phrases from the Exodus play as well as the character Tubal in Josephus's Antiquities of the Jews. Looking further into the insight Josephus, the writes of the Essene community made me wonder, did Josephus have a historical and personal link to the Essenes?

Josephus excelled in his studies of Jewish law and studied with the Sadducees, Pharisees, and the Essenes. Although eventually selecting and becoming a Rabbi of the Pharisees, a life to what was similar to his royal upbringing, his in-depth study and respect of the spiritual and materialistic lifestyle would not escape his respect. Keenly understanding that the Romans initially would not focus on the "hippie" lifestyle of the Essenes, Josephus knew at some point the devout commitment to the Mosaic laws would clash with the pagan belief and lifestyle of the Romans.

At the age of 16, he was not content with his studies, and for three years, he lived in the desert with a hermit named *Bannus*. The term *Banna* means housebuilder, likely in a rural area, this significant for it provided a dwelling for spiritual growth in a time when the rural desert meant wilderness. It was in this dwelling that

Bannus taught the philosophy of the intimate relationship between nature and spirituality, this Oneness connection that the Creator desired for all of humankind to understand, that was shared with Josephus.

Josephus studied with Bannus for over a three year period, until the age of nineteen, he decided to return to his affluent and educated lifestyle in Jerusalem and once again began the study of the Pharisees. He later became a Rabbi, yet never lost sight of the training by Bannus and the pride he kept for the understanding of the Essene spirituality of the *Truth of Israel*. Thus rendering Josephus a cryptic Essene.

With this knowledge insight, Josephus included significant themes in his writing to conceal his connection to the Essenes:

1. Languages of Aramaic and Paleo Hebrew
Josephus did not share with his Roman supervisors of historical research and writings of that time period, that he likely spoke *Siriac* (Aramaic) and Paleo Hebrew, this learned while a teen when studying and living with Bannus in the desert. The knowledge of the Essenes would have been prevented to be transferred to Josephus without the grasp of the Aramaic language of the esoteric concepts he was trained upon and shared.

2. Use of Dreams to Foretell Future Events
The use of dreams was made model by Daniel in relationship with King Nebuchadnezzar.

To share foresight of future events of both General Vespasian and his son Titus would become Emperor of Rome.

3. Dreams, Visions and Future

Auditory message dreams to tell a story and Visual Symbolic Dreams.

The auditory dream example is used dreams provide a vision of future to Roman General Vespasian that soon he would be Roman Emperor. This vision did come to pass and Vespasian became Emperor.

The spiritual dream in Josephus writings is *but was a kind of image of the universe; for by the scarlet there seemed to be enigmatically signified fire, by the fine flax the earth, by the blue the air, and by the purple the sea; two of them having their colors the foundation of this resemblance.* (Antiquities, Description of the Temple, 5-4)

4. Worship and Use of Angels as Messengers

Josephus knowledge that the Essenes's "worshipped" angels in direct conflict of the teaching of Mosaic laws. Utilized specific "names of angels," to be used as a messenger to bring particularly preserved by the Essene " to bring, them the peculiar books of their sectarian focus of the Elders such as Genesis, Enoch, Exodus, Daniel, Isiah, Job, and Tobit."

More specifically, as an example of how Josephus explained the use of an angel, *he ordered the messengers to tell it to the king*—utilized an angel as a messenger to deliver a message.

5. Josephus was aware of both a Lunar and Solar-Zodiac Calendar

The Essenes fixed the use of both the Lunar and Solar-Zodiac Calendar so that holidays do not fall on the Sabbath.

Furthermore, in an example of exoteric knowledge, Josephus writes, *In the month of Xanthicus, which is by us called Nisan, and is the beginning of our year, on the fourteenth day of the lunar month, when the sun is in Aries.* This demonstrates, both his knowledge of the lunar month and solar calendar year.

6. Cognizant of Tubal the Grandson of Noah
Historical link to Noah, in Josephus writing he states the description of his grandson Tubal as the *first of all invented the art of making brass*. An important historical figure that employed an advanced technology of that time.

Josephus mention of the Great Flood in the times of Noah and the mention of his grandson Tubal, a character in the Exodus play, demonstrate the association of the historical link to the Ages of sacred scriptures.

Noah comes to the beginning of the Age of Aries (100 BC-2000 BC), and the cataclysmic flood-deluge arrived with the preparation of the Ark. Noah prepared the boarding following sacred scriptures, *male and female created He them (Gen. i, 27)* and entered two by two.

In the Exodus play, the sole Judaic character Tubal, grandson of Noah, is the link to Creation and the survival of humankind.

Second Link to Creation

The Genesis story of the Fall, Adam and Eve story told by Josephus, shares of knowledge of both *Trees of Life-Good* and *Tree of Knowledge-Evil*. The story shares *the Fall* of the Devil as he Falls from heaven to be an angel of evil.

> *Adam and his wife should eat of all the rest of the plants, but to abstain from the tree of knowledge; and foretold to them, that if they touched it, it would prove their destruction. When they disobeyed them, they would fall into calamities..*

In the Exodus play, the unhappy Sephardic Hermanos, tell the story of *The Fall* from El Diablo-Devils point of view, sharing a contrarian Genesis story by use of the devil to tell of what the Sephardim encountered as genuine persons of faith.

Similar to the Essene's view that spiritual understanding of faith is the *True Israel*, the Exodus story is the in-depth understanding of the Genesis Fall story, is a genuine story commitment of *real faith*.

Josephus believes Jesus of Nazareth was Christ and aware Josephus was aware that the Nazarene was spiritually trained as an Essene. Both are representing the spiritualty of the Essene's.

7. Esoteric Knowledge of the Cosmos

The phrase, *Sun took with the moon* (Antiquities 2-2 and Exodus Play page 212) are both in Josephus's *Antiquities of the Jews* book and the Exodus play referred to the understanding that the Sun controlled the universe including the Moon and Earth. This early

Jewish mystical thought shared the universal knowledge that the Sun was the center of the universe when other astrophysical persons thought the Earth was central to the universe. This phrase among the writings of the Exodus play.

8. Future Cryptic Concept Used by Sephardic Jews to link to Josephus

---

The phrase, declared the future happiness of his son, is used by the Sephardic Ladino brothers as a camouflaged reference to Josephus meaning, Happy New Year of Yom Kippur in the Exodus play.

---

9. Understanding of the Tree of Knowledge

Both Flavius Josephus and the Genesis writings of Dead Sea Scrolls, share the same understanding of this essential concept of humanity. Josephus and the Essenes understood that the Tree of Knowledge was both good and evil. A conscious choice point was the key to this understanding. If one listened and did not eat from the forbidden tree, then good would ensue, if one did not listen and followed the Tree of Life and Evil and ate from the tree as did Adam, then destruction followed or the event of Noah's flood ensued.

For the Essenes, the Aramaic written book of Genesis was a favorite study book and was well preserved as an Essene property in Cave 3, very close to the Masada fort.

For Josephus, describing the Tree of Knowledge as both Good and Evil supports the philosophy of the sole Tree of Knowledge originating from one Creator.

Later, the Tree of Knowledge was adapted by the Kabbalah Zohar practice and became part of the origination of the Aramaic written Tree of Life study in Spain in the early 1300s.

10. Esoteric Values and Knowledge was kept Concealed

The Essenes study and commitment to esoteric values and knowledge was kept internally among only closely-held members that valued cosmic enlightenment, the interest and focused by members that Aramaic (known as Syriac dialect in Judea at that time) language was a primary impetus for the wisdom to be passed on throughout generations.

The primary language in a primary rural area was Aramaic, this language was established for the terminology utilized by Judaic mystics in their esoteric knowledge of the cosmos. This language predated by the less educated and backcountry rural sheepherders and farmers that spoke the original Paleo Hebrew and studied the Cosmos.

Josephus writes of the Aramaic as the Syriac language of which he learned as a teenager studying the Essenes, in his quest to understand the nuances of its philosophy and innermost wisdom and training. Josephus concealed his understanding of the language and philosophy from his Roman counterparts to preserve the insight of the Essenes. This demonstrated his Essene wisdom, as other writers of this era, such as Pines, wrote little of the detailed insight of the Essenes.

This concept was further verified when the writings of the Kabbalah and Zohar were written entirely in Aramaic in 13th century Spain. Flourishing in Spain, it was later concealed and utilized to conceal the cryptic Jews from the Spanish Diaspora to the present day in New Spain. (American Southwest)

This the primary factor that phrases from Josephus writings were concealed within the Exodus play in the mid-17th century.

11. Adaptation meant Survival

Josephus, at age 16, left home and joined to study and immerse himself in the study to be an Essene. Later he becomes a Rabbi and upon the intrusion of the Roman-Kitta, he became a war General in the uprising against the invader. Upon his capture, he reinvented himself to become the historian of the Roman war in Judea and later become a Roman citizen. Adaptation meant survival, similar to the Ladino community of New Mexico and southern Colorado. Yet he never forgot his roots of *True Israel* and the Essene Community.

Conclusion

Josephus maintaining the education and training from his young adult studies illustrates that he never relinquished his interest in his desire to be an Essene. His ability to use the Aramaic language to understand the philosophy and innermost wisdom of the Essenes demonstrated his unique knowledge of the brotherhood. Josephus ability to explain esoteric values and use of angels, dreams and visions provides for the determination that he privately thought of himself as an Essene. His ability to conceal and maintain his cryptic knowledge further demonstrates his invisible connection similar to the inner core values of the Essenes.

The uniquely writing of the Lunar and solar calendar, the Great Flood of Noah, the Tree of Life with Creation and his mention of his grandson Tubal (as with the Exodus Play) shares a singular inner knowledge of the importance lessens valued of Essenes. His belief furthermore that Jesus of Nazareth shared the Spirituality of the Essenes validates his own beliefs in the Essene community.

4

Who were the Original Esoteric Essenes
Esoteric Matter in Scrolls

The Essenes were famed for their esoteric knowledge of the healing arts and this has long been suggested as the real meaning of their name.

Literally, the "Essene" goes back to a *Sumerian* word meaning "diviner" and was borrowed into ancient *Akkadian* and thence into Aramaic and the other Semitic dialects with the meaning of "wonder-worker" and thus "physician." The ancient medicine man was, of course, basically a magician, combining a rudimentary knowledge of physiology with the practice of herbalism and general hocus-pocus. By his secret knowledge and rites, he obtained power over the devils that caused bodily and mental sickness.

They were celibates, apolitical mystics, and ascetics, much like those living in the Qumran caves, or they were revolutionaries, some were married, and some lived in Jerusalem. Experts in the healing of body and soul, they also excelled in prophecy. Their esoteric teachings were recorded in secret books, yet the discovery of the Qumran scrolls has made a few of their esoteric attributes available to readers.

Convinced that they belonged to a Community which alone interpreted the Holy Scriptures correctly, theirs was 'the last interpretation of the Law.' They devoted their exile in the wilderness to the study of the Bible. Their intention was to do according to all that had been 'revealed from age to age'.

As Healers, recognized as experts in the healing of body and soul, they also excelled in prophecy. They preferred belief in Fate to freedom of the will and, rejecting the notion of bodily resurrection, envisaged a purely spiritual afterlife.

Since Qumran and early Christianity partly overlap, it is easily recognizable to notice the healing techniques used by Christians originated with the organic healing capabilities of the Essenes.

Watchers

The esoteric thinking Essenes called a specific type of angel Watchers. The allusion is made to his writing activity, including astronomical knowledge, which was to stop the righteous from going astray. The two small fragments of 4Q227 contain references to both Moses and Enoch.

Giants

The mingling of fallen angels and humans created the Nephilim or Giant. The offspring of these unnatural unions were giants of great height. In the Book of Enoch, the fallen angels and the giants began to oppress the human population and to teach them to do evil. For this reason, God brought about Noah's Great Flood and imprisoned the fallen angels until the final judgment.

The Two Spirits
The earliest Jewish theological tractate incorporated into the Community Rule, the recognition of the Two Spirits, those of the Light and Dark Light.

Sons of Darkness is are considered enemies of Israel. They attract the virtues of Darkness, foolish, wicked, death and perdition, belong to Belial-devil, are the Roman-Kitta. The children of injustice are ruled by the Angel of Darkness and walk in the ways of darkness.

The Sons of Light are children of righteousness, ruled by the Prince of Light and walk in the ways of light. The Son of Light and the exiles from the desert, considered will go to the light, shine and defeat the Sons of Dark. Special Note, Faith of Light and Belief is NOT based on Skin Color, rather one's belief of the ways of light.

> *Faith of Light and Belief is NOT based on Skin Color, rather one's belief of the ways of light.*

Commanded by the 'Prince of the Congregation' were to be supported by the angelic armies led by the 'Prince of Light,' also known in the Scrolls as the archangel Michael or *Melchizedek*.

The Essenes at the beginning of the age of Pisces, asked the Prince of the Congregation to drive out the Roman-Kitta. ... [the Pr]ince of the congregation [will pursue them] as far as the [Great] Sea ... [and they shall fle] e from before Israel. (Vermes 4Q285,

FR. 4) Similarly, the Sephardic-Ladinos request the new Messiah to battle and defeat the Corporate Elite and Artificial Intelligence.

Considered Themselves the Remnant of Their Time

Not only did the Essenes considered themselves to be the '**remnant' of their time, but the 'remnant' of all time**, the final 'remnant.' In the 'age of wrath,' while God was making ready to annihilate the wicked, their founders had repented. They had become the 'Converts of Israel' (Vermes cf. CD IV, 2; 4Q266 fr. 5 i). As a reward for their conversion, the Teacher of Righteousness had been sent to establish for them a 'new Covenant,' which was to be the sole valid form of the eternal alliance between God and Israel. Consequently, their paramount aim was to pledge themselves to observe its precepts with absolute faithfulness. Convinced that they belonged to a Community which alone interpreted the Holy Scriptures correctly, theirs was 'the last interpretation of the Law' (Vermes 4Q266 fr. 11; 270 fr. 7 ii), and they devoted their exile in the wilderness to the study of the true law of Moses. Their intention was to do according to all that had been 'revealed from age to age'.

> *'the last interpretation of the Law' (Vermes 4Q266 fr. 11; 270 fr. 7 ii), and they devoted their exile in the wilderness to the study of the true law of Moses.*

The number of 364 days is neatly divided by seven, a typological number with significant religious connotation, following a Solar Calendar. Each 364-day year contains exactly fifty-two weeks, a fact that allows anchoring the festivals to fixed weekdays, thus avoiding their coincidence with the Sabbath.

The Book of Daniel

The Essene use of dreams and visions is similar to esoteric mysteries that are revealed is the ability to further study the writings of the books that contain mystical or obscure knowledge used by the prophet Daniel. Early Judaism presents mystery as a revelation concerning end-time events that were previously hidden but have been subsequently revealed with the Qumran scrolls.

What has not changed is that to gain the mystical insight, the immersion and study of scripture is the key to obtain the esoteric concepts. To understand visions, one must be able to interpret dreams granted by the light of the Creator itself.

Similarly, in the Second dream vision of the Book of Enoch (90 2-25), the Essene authors once again make use of the auto antonym-dual meaning of eloquence, the use of animals to represent human beings and human beings to represent angels, *the eagles led all the birds; and they began to devour those sheep, and to pick out their eyes.*

Water

For the Essenes, water calms their soul bathing twice daily, the cistern system that channeled water was considered miraculous for it was here that esoteric thoughts and matters were discussed and debated.

The Masada Fortress was filled from underground virgin water springs that brought water in from the high end of the elevated lands, then run through various channels to fill cisterns to be used early in the morning and then released for new waters to fill cisterns in the evening after chores or studies were completed.

This frequent bathing brought forward the cleansing of both body and soul for the genuine prayer studies and thought to be procured.

Aramaic Speaking Essenes

The Aramaic speaking Essenes were especially attuned of study what was called then the Astrology of the cosmos. This group focused and wrote of the cosmic matters available as time tested observations. Living in very rural areas, they observed and studied the concepts of Pursued Wisdom of Spring and Fall Equinox, Celestial Equator and Astronomy Age Timing, Search

> *Aramaic speaking Essenes contains cryptic arithmetic counts or signals not yet uncovered in terms of their cosmic knowledge that await disclosure.*

for Original Heaven, Sun in Taurus hoof to begin planting season, Solar and Lunar Eclipse, Arithmetic counts to locate star patterns and configurations.

There also remains the possibility that the Copper Scrolls likely were written by the Aramaic speaking Essenes contains cryptic arithmetic counts or signals not yet uncovered in terms of their cosmic knowledge that await disclosure.

Higher Dimensional Thinking

The advanced astrological thinking of the Aramaic influenced Essenes, provided the pathway for the creation of the Kabbalah in

Iberian Spain and then later for the Latino influenced writings in New Spain shared in the writings, *Shared Lives, Twin Sun*.

The search and discover of original Heaven known as *Semano*, known as the *First Sun* of the Milky Way and amniotic sack termed *Firmament*. Time travel via the use of the Portal of Light via the use of Plank-Strand Technology, Plank Propulsion System, AntiGravitation Matter.

This is originating from the knowledge of the Light and Dark Light of the Essenes that manifested into the Manipulation of Light and Dark Matter, Cosmic Time of the Fourth Dimension and Arithmetic counts to locate star configuration.

Ascension and The Essenes

The Book of Enoch once again provides a unique perspective of the ascension to the celestial realm above Earth, known as Heaven. Engaging the creative interweave of the simultaneous application of Angels, Portals Visions and Dreams.

The Essenes did believe in the Holy Spirit, and they devoted their exile in the wilderness to the study of the Bible. Their intention was to do according to all that had been revealed, devoted their exile in the wilderness to the study of the Bible. Their intention was to do according to all that had been 'revealed from age to age, and as the Prophets had revealed by His Holy Spirit. (Vermes 1QS VIII, 14– 16; cf. 4Q265 fr. 7 ii).

The fascinating Essene view is the belief and conceptualization of the Human transformation into a Celestial Angel. The Essenes applied the angel Uriel as the Time Traveler, visiting different Ages or Time Frames and using Portals to enter these Ages of Time Frames.

Shockingly to this author, it is with this concept that the character *Hermitaño* was used as Time Traveler landing in the Time Frame to join the Shepherds in visiting the birth cave of the Jesus of Nazareth.

The concept of the Portal as a window into another Time Frame, the Portal of Light followed by the shepherds to locate the birth cave of Jesus of Nazareth. The borrowing of the use of the Portal demonstrates the celestial grasp of esoteric concepts the writers of the Exodus play possessed.

The alien hybrid of part man-beast was the creation of the Giants sent from the above to Earth. Considered a myth in the writings of the Essenes, there are some that have witnessed such a being in today's territory along the 33° parallel in the American Southwest.

5

Messianic Conception:
The Mark of The Covenant

The illustrative demonstration of faith and obedience to God is what will continue real faith, and this was demonstrated in the cryptic Alabado, *Salbe Luna Hermana-Save the Sister Moon*, concealed within its writings was the prose:

"Give glory and great enjoyment in the name of the Mark"
(stanza 6) a very unique line in a Christian Alabado that refers directly to the Torah's Joshua 5, Circumcision will be a mark of the Covenant between God and Man.
Source: Shared Lives, Twin Sun

It is with this demonstration of Judaic faith that the surviving Ladino families persevered and stood in reverence for the most high relationship between God and Humankind in the expectation that one day in the future, they will be rewarded for this historic faith and the knowledge that a new Messiah-*Mashiach, the Anointed One*, will arrive in the Age of Aquarius.

This is the level of commitment exhibited by the Ladino families of real faith that is required to survive in the times of the Corporate Elite and AI.

Are the Elements in Place for The Advent of The Messiah in The Age of Aquarius?

The Sephardic community arrived in New Spain after the Expulsion of 1492. The soldiers and families joined expeditions or caravans to the outermost northern location of the Spanish empire. The journey was lengthy, all the while concealed as the cryptic Jews, most trained in the Law of Moses, others also aware of the Kabbalah.

The Jewish families understood the religious fervor that swept across the Iberian peninsula, yet they hoped that the Monarchy of New Spain would accept Jesus of Nazareth as part of the continued relationship of Jewish history. This known as the Continuum. This was never considered an acceptable option.

In New Spain concealed for over four centuries, the expelled families would outwardly be devout Catholics, inwardly or privately at home they would not relinquish or renounce the faith of their family like Judah. Secret services, cryptic prayers, kosher meals and camouflage strategies were developed to conceal their faith as many resided in secluded rural parts of a community.

Many Sephardic Jews felt God was punishing them for the duel faith life many have led. Faith is a funny concept, the rewards sometimes to be awaited decades, centuries, or a millennium. Yet the Sephardim in New Spain preferred the name las *Seranitas*. They would retain the knowledge of a significant future event as a reward of this faith, this a direct lesson believed by the original Essenes. The *Seranitas* were aware soon the coming of the new Age of Aquarius would arrive in the year 2012 and a transcendental opportunity for a new Messiah to arrive as part of this new age.

The Exodus play was requested to be made public and decoded. The story of a Community repressed for now centuries would certainly be deserving from the Lord, the request that the future Mary be born the Messiah.

The Play itself would garnish little interest or a book written on the Play, most certainly be banned by media, arts, theatre, libraries and the general community as a whole would ignore such nonsense of philosophy. The formal religious community would certainly question the story's validity. Yet, one thing was sure, the Essenes prayed and requested for an earth-born Messiah and were granted Jesus of Nazareth.

Just as in the time of the Essenes, the elders were aware that the forthcoming armies of the Roman-Kitta, would sack the Temples and eradicate Judaic culture and remove worship, the expected list anticipatory of events were disregarded with the arrival of Jesus of Nazareth.

The Age of Aquarius will bring foreword a similar Kitta, known as the Corporate Elite and AI, the repression and control of these entities will again require the list of prior events to be overlooked due to the might of the present Kitta.

This Age of Aquarius will provide the window of opportunity for the Messiah-*Mashiach* to arrive for it will be most needed and imperative to defeat both the Corporate Elite and their primary ally of Artificial Intelligence.

Are the Passive Prayers Requesting the Arrival of The Messiah Effective?

The Essenes maintained faith that the Lord would reward them for their *real faith* and study of the scrolls to be granted a Messiah. The Essenes's felt they were the *True Israel*, the authentic belief of the Lord, surpassing both Pharisee and Sadducees beliefs. This term did not arrive without effort, and the scrolls were studied and applied to their lives, foregoing all material goods and bonding with nature in spirituality. It was expected that the earthborn Messiah child would be granted to this community.

> *It was expected that the earthborn Messiah child would be granted to this community.*

The Sephardic Jews feel that their sacrifice and repression, their genuine prayers will be granted a Messiah in the Age of Aquarius. Prayers from the Sephardim in New Spain, are presented in two forms. Direct prayers to the Lord, requesting that the need for a dual faith be lifted from their shoulders. The second is placed cryptically in the songs of praise Alabados that is specifically shared between Brothers of Light. The Creator will reward perseverance of faith from this repression, with the insight knowledge of the coming Emmanuel.

How is the next Mary to be Treated?

For both the Essenes and Brothers of Light, an angel, Uriel or the Hermitaño is brought forward to tell of the story of time travel and of things to come to the community. An angel will likely inform an earthborn Mother that she is to carry a child that will be the new Messiah.

Optimally, AI and the non-Believes should not be shared with the notice that the Mother of the Messiah has been informed of her upcoming role. A quiet birthing process and a loving family atmosphere would be best for the mother and child.

AI will be on constant vigilance for any word pertaining to Messiah, and like Herod will attempt to hunt such a child. AI's methods of surveillance will be vast, sophisticated listening devices, incentive paid informers in many corners of all communities.

Yet the Sephardim will know how to "cloak" or make invisible both the Mother and Child. Membership in concealing themselves for hundreds of years has its benefits.

Whom Will Request the Messiah to Arrive in the Era of Aquarius?

The Brothers of Light, the Ladino Hermanos Penitentes have requested the earthborn Messiah to be born. The prayers will be answered for the innocent of heart. Las *Seranitas* have kept their faith in the Law of Moses, belief in One God and comported themselves as respectable persons of faith in an environment hostile to their beliefs. They have concealed the history of the Jews and fought against those of hatred of real faith and anti-Creation.

The non-Believes and the technology of Artificial Intelligence will certainly have taken hold of modern society. AI will craftily listen and pursue the new Mother Mary using sophisticated listening and tracking devices. AI's objective will be to abduct the New Messiah and see if possible to turn this child into believing the philosophy of AI and the non-believers. If not, the new Messiah life will be terminated. Interestingly, at the time the early first century, the age of early Pisces, the pursuer was named King Herod ruthlessly slaughtered newborns. Imagine a time where all of your personal and governmental details are gathered to track your interests and associates, the use of Facebook, Twitter and cell phone usage and location monitor all of your movements. The Corporate Elite can easily monitor all of actions and anticipate your next movement.

The Corporate Elite may not permit a One person spokesperson or leader, but rather a board of directors whose names are undisclosed. Life to this board of directors is just a sterile and faithless, none the less, this board and followers should be held responsible for their decisions and actions for repressing and threatening the life and community of the New Messiah.

The Time of The Arrival of The New Messiah Will Not Be Disclosed.

The New Mary identity will not be disclosed as well as the potential date of birth of the New Messiah. This to provide for a safe environment for the proper upbringing for the new child Messiah. There remains a possibility that the Sephardim community that is familiar with concealment practices may be asked to conceal the sacred family. It would be an honor for the *Serananitas* to assist in concealing and educating the young Messiah.

> *The New Mary identity will not be disclosed as well as the potential date of birth of the New Messiah.*

What did the Essenes Believe as the Possibility of the Arrival of a Messiah?

There were two schools of thought within the Essene group.

While most of the Essenes were pacifist by nature, the expected child born Messiah was to reflect those values of healing, spirituality, faith, study and prayer, similar in nature of their brotherhood. For many followers and those that would be in fact, the first Christians, they believed Jesus of Nazareth to be a real Messiah described as the *Lamb of God*.

The second school of thought was of those Essenes who believed in defending the Masada fort and contributed to the writing of the War Scrolls:

[the Prin] ce of the Congregation and all Is[rael] ... [which wa] s written [in the book of Ezekiel the Prophet, I will strike your bow from your left hand and will make your arrows drop from your right hand.] On the mountains of [Israel you shall fall] ... [the king of] the Kittim ... [the Pr] ince of the congregation [will pursue them] as far as the [Great] Sea ... [and they shall fle] e from before Israel. In that time ... he shall stand against them and they shall be stirred against them ... and they shall return to the dry land. In that time ... and they shall bring him (the king of the Kittim?) before the Prince.. (Vermes 4Q285, Fr 4...)

The Price of the Congregation described above is likely the adult Messiah type the Pharisee community was awaiting, a Messiah that will strike the Kitta-Romans with bows and arrow and defeat the invading army.

The Roman-Kitta did siege and sack the Temples in Jerusalem and forever change the life of all of Judea and this leads to the question, what type of skill set must the Messiah possess to counter AI and the Corporate Elite and what are we to expect in the next Age of Aquarius?

The New Messiah-*Mashiach* Pacifist or Warrior

Just as the Essene community was faced with the dilemma of how to defend against the fast-approaching Roman-Kitta, the question arose, will the new Messiah be a Pacifist or a leader Warrior type? The solution to this question would be the answer by the not identified person mentioned in the scrolls, *the Teacher of Righteousness, to whom God made known all the mysteries* (Vermes 1QpHab VII, 1- 5). This teacher was never fully disclosed and never identified. Various historians think of this person as the "wicked priest", or leader of the Essenes, and others Jesus of Nazareth.

It will be fascinating to witness the type of Messiah the Lord brings forward in the Age of Aquarius in the twenty-first century. The answer may lie in the strength of the Corporate Elites, AI, and their non-Believing followers. A second important factor that will influence the type of Messiah that is to arrive is in the prayers and requests by the genuine Believers.

The Role of Women at the Beginning of New Age Aquarius

How is She the Next Mary to be Treated?

Women Maintain a Crucial Role in the Relationship to Creation.

It is no coincidence that the Creation Technology of abortions, birth control, synthetic children and body parts and decisions to embrace same-sex relationships appear at the doorstep just prior to the entrance into the Age of Aquarius in the year 2012. Women were meant to be a crucial part of the Age of Aquarius.

The entrance of these technologies play a significant role for it affects the relationship with Creation itself. Historically it was thought that only God itself could create children and heal body illnesses or body parts. It is now thought of as a choice to create children or a choice to heal an illness or body part.

Creation Technology

Women play a key role in these decisions, the women gender is challenging the role of the Creator in many ways for they are able to carry the child or possibly a synthetic embryo is placed within a woman and carried to term or may terminate a pregnancy. This shall now be identified as Creation Technology.

This role is significant for the new Messiah will arrive based on the time frame that challenges the existence of the Creator itself. If synthetic armies can be built or a synthetic child or body part that can be developed within a women's body, this is a direct challenge to the historical existence of the Creator. Women will play a significant role in the arrival of the Messiah.

The interesting parallel of Creation Technology and the growth of same-sex relationships will play a significant factor in this next age. The Corporate Elite will embrace both of these groups and rely on these two factions to fuel their acceptance and importance in the next age.

How Will Women Play a Part in the Future Messiah

How will Women play a part in the future Messiah? By understanding their role in crucial points of decisions in the Aquarius Age. By awakening and understanding that Women's Rights and decisions over their bodies has been abused as a crutch to justify the values and decisions of the Corporate Elite and AI. Just accepting new technologies that affect the body of a women without thought of its impact will reflect on how the *Next Mary is to be Treated*.

Imagine a time when the power of the Corporate Elite and AI is unlimited and they are able to approximate a time that a new Messiah is to be born on a specific and date, time and location. The Corporate Elite understands clearly that this event will jeopardize their very existence and know they possess the technology to rid such a risk and continue their dominance.

A new Creation Technology application named *The Day After Pill*, may terminate a pregnancy 24 hours after conception is what may likely be used on a group of women to prevent the conception of the next Messiah. When the Corporate Elite feel confident that the new Messiah has been conceived in a particular genre or location of a group of women, they will enforce their capability to prevent this pregnancy and forcibly require all eligible pregnancy women between the age of 17-47 report to a certain location begin the process to take this pill.

A second option would require all pregnant women from a particular region and time and date, be required to obtain abortions to avoid the new Messiah from being born.

The Biblical story of the bloody slaughter of children of modern-day would be far too evasive when a Pill or an Abortion would be more sterile and in line of with modern thinking with the use of techniques, the Corporate Elite will utilize.

One may think this is not plausible in the modern day? The genocide atrocities of European Bosnia and African Barfur are the most recently recorded events.

Do not underestimate the strength and influence that the Corporate Elite will maintain and the ability to use an AI skillset as a pill or an abortion to rid the challenge of their existence by use of technology. The Elite will provide camouflage marketing campaigns to conceal their real objectives and values. The death of a Messiah will be viewed as an expiration of a rival without explanation.

Women must think outside of the box of specifically how their bodies will be manipulated, not the immediate benefit preventing an unwanted pregnancy when endorsing such a technology that provides such widespread future applications. Women are the key to grasping the future concepts of *how the Next Mary is to be Treated* and the birth of the next earthborn Messiah.

The New Messiah's Values and Beliefs

The Messiah will always align with the values of Creation, the Genesis of Adam and Eve, this axiom has never changed throughout all of the Ages. This axiom is a central part of the tenet of a continual relationship beginning from the original scrolls maintained by the Essenes, then the laws granted in the Torah to then flowing to the advent of Christianity.

Yet the most significant value that the new Messiah will bring forward is Hope. Hope provides the Spirit to stand up to the Corporate Elite at any price.   This is what the Elite fear most, for the spirit will give the valor to question Elite policies and motives. The Corporate Elite understands that the Genesis story is not acceptable to their existence. The Elite moved away from these historic axioms to separate from these old church views and brand themselves as the future, never thinking of the advent of a new Messiah. The Elite will scorch the earth in search of either the Mother Mary or the existence of the new Messiah. The Corporate Elite possesses the technology to prevent the advent of the new Mary and terminate the birth of the next Messiah. Will they present world-wide community options to prevent the existence of the new Messiah, just as Herod killed all newborns under the age of two?

A Women's Decision Will Determine the Lamb of God or Warrior Messiah

Interestingly, women must, at some point, understand that their decisions to support Creation Technology and Same-Sex relationships will have an impact on the type of Messiah that will arrive. Both of these axioms will not support the philosophy of the original Creation of Adam and Eve.

With the advent of knowledge of the arrival Time Frame for the new Messiah, there is a window for both organically and parent trained children to possess family values of the school of Creation. Women's role as a primary caregiver of children can contribute greatly to society to form child values that match with those of the new Messiah. The current anti-family and Creation Technology philosophy taught in public schools is the antithesis of the personal values the new Messiah will possess.

What is certain is a paradigm that will present itself, is the next Messiah going to be a *Lamb of God* or a *Warrior Messiah*? Either type of Messiah will support the philosophy of the original Creation, yet women as a whole can influence society in raising their children to understand the importance of original Creation and its connection to the new Messiah. A society that is accepting and open to the expected existence of the new Messiah will create a loving environment for the Lamb of God Messiah to exist and work within.

The pacifist Messiah will follow the philosophies of the healing nature of the Essenes and the astrology virtues of Aquarius, that being a leader of love, brotherhood, unity and integrity. The Believers will be born and trained with the knowledge of the spiritual mystics of the Essenes, later passed on as the Kabbalah wisdom from the middle-ages and now is expected to compete with AI in the Age of Aquarius. Will this healing nature compete or maybe be able to coexist with the cold and analytical decision based philosophy and repression of AI and the Corporate Elite?

This creates the ultimate enigma, will the Corporate Elite and AI be able to dominate the nature of this Warrior Messiah? The Warrior Messiah will follow the writings of the Torah, the Law of Moses and the possible End of Days scenario. A battle for existence will be led by the Warrior Messiah against the Non-Believers Corporate Elite and AI.

Will either the Pacifist or Warrior Messiah and their religious and historical values of competitive spirit and toughness, be sufficient to survive in the twenty-first century? These are these iconic virtues of real faith of the past, the wisdom of the original Creator now foregone by many, survive in a technologically advanced society?

The New Messiah Will be Known as The Anointed One

The Hebrew word Yeshua *HaMashiach*, is the literal translation meaning Messiah, describing a future savior person to come. The Hebrew word *Mashiach* comes from the root Mem-Shin-Chen, which means to paint, smear, or anoint, refers to the ancient practice of anointing kings with oil when they took the throne. The *Mashiach* is the one who will be anointed as king in the End of Days.

The word *Moshiah* comes from the root Yod-Shin-Ayin, which means to help or save. This the determinant of the Essenes values as Healers or to Save as in Savior. The Divine or semi-Divine being who will sacrifice himself to save us from the consequences of our own sins is a Christian concept.

The uniqueness of the new Messiah, the new Anointed One, is the ability to recognize the influence and contributions by Jesus of Nazarene and work with Believers in this Age of Aquarius.

The *Mashiach*, whose translation is the translation that will used as the Anointed One in this writing to refer to the new Messiah in the 21st Century.

With the above stated, as the Essenes clearly understood the future rapture, the arrival of the Anointed One will take precedence over the lengthy list of *When will the Messiah Come* and *What will the Messiah do* questions of drama that unfolds.

6

Artificial Intelligence
The Real Enemy of Conscious Thought

In the Age of Aquarius, the time of the twenty-first and twenty second centuries, research and development work in Artificial Intelligence (AI) is split between two branches. One is labeled "applied AI," which uses these principles of simulating human thought to carry out one specific task.

The other is known as "generalized AI," which seeks to develop machine intelligence that can turn their hands to any task, much like a person.

AI will be controlled by those known as the Corporate Elite; they will be identified as the Scientific, Intellectual, Engineering, Managerial and Financial elites that control Wall Street, London, Tokyo, Beijing and all major financial cities. All of the Elites will possess locator tags for identification under the skin of their forearm. Corporate Elite share specific recognizable traits of being connected to the development of liberal corporate values

> *the Corporate Elite; they will be identified as the Scientific, Intellectual, Engineering, Managerial and Financial elites that control Wall Street*

but possessing few religious values, which often translates into their being unable or unwilling to create children organically. Their focus on a career track in lieu of spouse or family and volunteering in order to create dependency, place themselves in positions of influence.

Applied AI

Research into applied, specialized AI is already providing breakthroughs in fields of study from quantum physics, where it is used to model and predict the behavior of systems comprised of billions of subatomic particles, to medicine where it is being used to diagnose patients based on genomic data.

In industry, it is employed in the financial world for uses ranging from fraud detection to improve customer service by predicting what services customers will need. In manufacturing, it is used to manage workforces and production processes as well as for predicting faults before they occur, therefore enabling predictive maintenance. Its most secret development is in the area of robotic coordination of patterning of human movements and capabilities via a robotic human genre that will permit the proficient skill level of humans to be copied by robotic imposters.

> *a robotic human genre that will permit the proficient skill level of humans to be copied by robotic imposters.*

In the consumer world, more and more of the technology we are adopting into our everyday lives is becoming powered by AI—from smartphone assistants like Apple's Siri and Google's Assistant to self-driving and autonomous cars, which many are predicting will outnumber manually driven cars within our lifetimes.

Generalized AI

Generalized AI is a bit further off—to carry out a complete simulation of the human brain would require both a more complete understanding of the organ than we currently have and more computing power than is commonly available to researchers. But that may not be the case for long, given the speed with which computer technology is evolving. A new generation of computer chip technology known as neuromorphic processors is being designed to more efficiently run brain-simulator code. And systems such as IBM's Watson cognitive computing platform use high-level simulations of human neurological processes to carry out an ever growing range of tasks without being explicitly taught how to do them.

Real fears that development of intelligence which equals or exceeds our own, but can work at far higher speeds, could have negative implications for the future of humanity have been voiced, and not just by apocalyptic sci-fi such as The Matrix or The Terminator, but respected scientists like Stephen Hawking. Hawking's view is that AI, may be "... the worst event in human history and it is best "... to employ best practice and effective management ..." to establish boundaries of usage for AI.

> The Matrix or The Terminator, but respected scientists like Stephen Hawking. Hawking's view is that AI, may be "... the worst event in human history and it is best "... to employ best practice and effective management ..." to establish boundaries of usage for AI.

Robots may have the capabilities to eradicate humans or turn us into living batteries, a less dramatic but still nightmarish scenario is that automation of labor (mental as well as physical) will lead to profound societal change. Human labor of any sort that is repetitive in nature, building electronic widgets, picking of strawberries, vacuuming of floors, cutting of lawns, will be entirely replaced by AI components. Those directly affected by their replacement by robotics will not initially possess the foresight to see their intrinsic value to society being replaced; this group will be cast aside except for their ability to reproduce offspring. Robotic founders and leadership will use humans as needed to bear and manage children to the age of three years old, then taken from family and raised children of AI.

Those families and children that accept AI leadership will be educated in private schools to promote and learn AI systems to assist in maintaining AI's leadership in society. This scenario will be entirely protected under the guise of civil rights laws as they stand today.

Language of AI

AI will be at the forefront of teaching the language of the future, a learning management system is a flexible synthesis of websites, apps, webcasts via the use of handheld devices that are taught day or night.

The dialect taught in English or Chinese is irrelevant; AI will concentrate on locating one common trait of their students, that individual trait is Selfishness.

It will be long forgotten in this selfish world of AI the most iconic phrase that embodied many a generation,

---

"Ask not what your country can do for you, ask what you can do for your country."
(President John F. Kennedy Inauguration Address 1961)

Have no doubt, the Elites will maintain the majority of the country's populace complacent financially and ignorant to their objectives while selecting a most *Selfish* and talented society that will conceal their applications and create and operate AI's vast Learning Management systems.

Who Will Embrace AI

As stated before, those who will embrace AI fall into a dichotomy of expressing liberal values over religious values while considering themselves persons of faith. Yet they support the creation of life in petri dishes and synthetically created body parts to support the swift repair of humans created in a lab while supporting the paired implementation of synthetic soldiers. They will be skillful in using civil rights laws and media to protect non-traditional family values and repress any form of art that links to traditional values by controlling decisions in libraries, public and social forums and classrooms across the educational field. Their acceptance of synthetic capabilities underlies a lack of human soul. These individuals create a band of similar collective traits that work in tandem to repress persons of real faith.

At first glance, AI technology advancement will be cute and stunning, but they will have a very different objective than raising families. Their spectacular settings of lush downtown offices and living in dazzling homes and condos will surely sway many followers. The upper-echelon art performers will be among their exclusive friends, and their ability to converse with and name-drop the high-level political and financial friends will surely remove any doubt as to their synthetic pathway of life.

This association that embraces AI will also possess a special skill, that is to use religious icons, as in titles or names of organizations or religious pictures of their organizations, as subterfuge or camouflage to imply their purpose is that of a real religious faith or has a pious organic basis. This band and its supporters should be kept in the special prayers by real believers; genuine persons of faith should never forget this band of nonbelievers, for they will rise to the height of power. They will be very resourceful at utilizing staff and volunteers of persons of faith to benefit the objectives of supporters of AI and the Corporate Elite, without the slightest care for the underlying values of common persons of faith or their real religious objectives.

The Corporate Elite's Faith

The Corporate Elite will emulate a similar form of society's mainstream Christian religions, yet have a different faith than that of the believers. The Corporate Elite comprehend that they must have a religious faith but conceal their beliefs in evolution as the premise of history. Their churches will possess no insignia of Christ on the cross, the Last Supper, Mary and the Emmanuel in

> *Their churches will possess no insignia of Christ on the cross, the Last Supper, Mary and the Emmanuel in the manger.*

the manger. Instead, scarfs of multiple colors that are similar to a rainbow will adorn the walls and balconies. The Elite's orators will quote lovely Christian sayings but will not acknowledge the commitment by Christians in battles and wars over tyranny. Faith-based values of the family will not be emphasized, just quietly ignored to justify their lifestyles that are not reflective of historic family values.

Judaic Faith and The Corporate Elite

Those members of the Judaic background that have embraced the Elite will create a new faith that embraces the Corporate Elite's belief systems. They may replace the term Rabbi with the more open-minded name of the Teacher. This Teacher will support non-traditional values and families and go one step further. The Elite followers will embrace a not-seated chariot as part of their faith, a Palace in heaven, to distinguish themselves from the Jewish believers that embrace a seated angel in the chariot descent. Those persons not familiar with the vast separation in belief will only recognize this as a cosmetic effect when *this symbol is the cornerstone belief of Judaic faith and the Essene community.*

The Corporate Elite will mislead their followers that the concept of Ezekiel's *chariot descent* links their belief in faith to the early Essenes as the *True Israel*. They will utilize the flawed story of Herkhalot version, whereas the vision of the chariot is not a vision, rather the vision is a Palace or a place; *the decent of the chariot does not culminate in a vision, but rather in the Merkavah mystic's participation in the heavenly liturgy.*

> *They will utilize the flawed story of Herkhalot*

> *This will be of a marked difference to the legitimate Yeridah Markalot vision of the chariot, the "Throne has been seated in Chariot" and that if the Chariot "Appears," it can be seen. To praise God, one must "See the Image of the Throned Chariot" as it descends.*

This differentiation is the key to understanding the *True Israel*, and how sacred scripture will be manipulated in the future for the benefit of the Corporate Elite.

Locating a Camouflaged AI: Separate the Signal From the Noise

Locating those persons or organizations that are genuine supporters of AI may, at times, be challenging. The impressive AI capabilities, valued pricing of services, marketing campaigns and support by influential persons in the community are the "Noise" that is the camouflage to conceal the true signal of AI.

It is imperative that one is vigilant and look deeper into the Noise. Influential people share the same mindset of AI itself and will champion marketing campaigns that will focus and highlight the efficiency and power of AI, ignoring the human values relinquished by following the AI mode lifestyle. Value pricing will bring advertisers to support AI and maintain same values as primary AI providers. The AI seduction and capabilities put in jeopardy conscious thinking for decisions.

Who Will Not Embrace AI?

Those with genuine religious faith, connected to the Creator of Earth as Genesis of Human Life, will be able to separate the camouflaged values of the Corporate Elite and understand boundaries for the use of AI for themselves and their family. Recognize that AI will use real humans that are complicit with AI technology to market their virtues, and these individuals will masquerade their true values that reflect those of the Corporate Elites. These believers will understand that dependency on AI will remove your conscious independent thoughts in exchange for usage of AI's technology and use real people complicit with AI technology to market its virtues. Those people will reflect no relationship to Creation or strong faith, no birth children, with objectives that masquerade their true values.

> *Recognize that AI will use real humans that are complicit with AI technology to market their virtues*

Those with a heightened awareness will realize that objectives of AI will be to make one dependent on it to solve life challenges, rather than going to family or friends for advice, AI's neuromorphic processors will provide detailed choices of audio and film options. AI seeks to remove the individual from reaching out to another human being for individual needs and remove the relationship between the conscious, real connection of humankind and God the Creator.

How Does AI Remove Conscious Thinking?

Applied interactive systems such as the AI of the IBM Watson's platform will be relied upon to answer the questions of "*Why?*" No longer will independent curiosity be used to answer the question of "Why?"

Solutions and analysis from the neuromorphic processor's units will be considered the complete answer to a question. Independent curiosity, a historical mainstay of human evolution, will no longer be a virtue, instead replaced by the control of the mind by AI.

The use of Google Assistant or Apple's Siri will be made available to the masses for less than $10.00 per month, creating dependence upon AI for all questions to be answered. This will also permit AI to control and limit the scope of options of answers to be provided and thus limit the critical thinking capabilities of humans.

The Corporate Elite will Masquerade Judaic-Christian Values

AI and Corporate Elite will no longer maintain the virtues and point of view of Judeo-Christian values that have been the historical pattern of thinking of many successful societies. Although the United States of America was founded upon the backbone of the historic values of faith in this country, AI values will reflect core values that provide for two factors: liberal global elite values and survival of AI as a priority.

Marketing and packaging the virtues of AI as the most effective and efficient form of lifestyle practice will be the cornerstone of their practice. The true objective of AI will be masked by the impressive capabilities of AI, while the real objective is to control conscious choices and the removal of curiosity in the human mind.

The Corporate Elite will maintain control over vast sections of industry and most corporate management will be dependent upon their technology in order to operate effectively. The Elite will go one step further, and covertly hire employees that will be accepting of the Elite values and informational control practices of this ruling entity.

How can AI Control Unconscious Thought?

AI will go one step further, and this is to influence or control unconscious thought. AI understands that real control of human consciousness must begin and end with the control of unconscious critical thinking.

When speaking a language for the first time, your consciousness is taking its time to remember words and conjugations to clarify and place order to respond in quick fashion. However, when you are practiced enough, you no longer have to think about what to say because your brain will naturally think in that language. That is your unconscious doing the work for you, without you even realizing it. Consciousness is the middle-man, and it doesn't do as much work as the critical thinking unconsciousness. AI recognizes this regular occurring phenomenon and realizes that its technology must access the unconscious to control the conscious of the human mind. Therefore, AI must place the vocabulary of words, analysis and point of view in a ready-made platform, accessed by the conscious mind as the database of information to be fed to the unconsciousness for critical thinking.

> *of human consciousness must begin and end with the control of unconscious critical thinking.*

In a simpler context, when the words and completed analysis by Apple's Siri act as the platform for an individual to access information, the unconscious—the brain—will now organically think in the language of Siri. It will process answers to give to the consciousness and unknowingly think in the form and manner of Siri or AI itself.

Job well done, by both AI and the Corporate Elite. Even more lovely, it is paid for by individuals and families that access Apple Siri or Google's Assistant, for it makes life easier and more efficient. Individuals surrender their consciousness and their critical thinking unconsciousness, unaware that their autonomy of analysis has been handed over to AI itself.

Channels the Answers to Questions That Disclose AI Philosophy

Today, even to look up a word definition, Google is the platform that provides the answer from the point of view of the decision-makers at Google. The answers provided may or may not be a dictionary definition; what *is* certain—Google controls the realm of solutions for millions of users. At the same time, advertisements will be placed to provide solutions to your question, on the margins to the side of the Google answer. Today, the solutions provided by Google are limited in scope and likely match the philosophy of the answer that accords with their corporate philosophy.

In the near future, it is to be expected that the Corporate Elite may someday own or control Google via their board of directors, and will influence the answers that reflect what the Corporate Elite wants you to know, and thus controls what you know.

Those very astute and questioning conscious thinkers will be identified by AI as "problem thinkers," and will be provided

> *AI's objective is to remove the knowledge capabilities from the "problem thinkers."*

finite answers to their questions and limited access to the web itself. AI's objective is to remove the knowledge capabilities from the "problem thinkers."

The Lost Generation

The Millennial, or Gen Y, ages of young adults born in or around 1981 to 1997, and Generation Post-Millennial, or Gen Z, born after 2002, are considered a Lost Generation by many parents and grandparents. This group of young adults has little interest in getting to know or respect the values of their parents or grandparents. Rather, hand-held games, laptop and desktop videos, and computer games garner their conscious and unconscious thought and values of importance.

This has resulted in a loss of the transfer of family history, any accomplishments of family elders and what they have stood for in society. This is a passive form of family dis-association; AI successfully removes the importance of family values and provides for the Millennial-age adults to question and reject historic family norms and their importance in life for themselves.

What many older American adults see are missing core values of the work ethic and consider the Millennial-age young as lazy, unfocused and not committed to traditional values. What is not recognized is that AI has removed the historic values of deferred gratification, sacrifice and work ethic, passed down from family, via the use of AI games that remove respect for the importance of parents and grandparents. Grandparents see that their grandchildren have no interest in their journey as elder family members and what they stand for.

A classic example of this generational disrespect is the Millennial age North American defector to Russia, Eric Snowden, who possesses the values of contempt and genuine dislike of our precious historical values of the United States of America. Snowden illustrates the values set of the Selfish Generation of the modern young adult, instead of placing emphasis upon the value of what their grandparents' generation signified.

What the Millennial/Gen Y and Post-Millennial/Gen Z ages have not comprehended is that AI will first replace white collar positions before blue collar positions, for it is much easier to replace an analyst or service person with a replicating AI droid and most Millennials occupy white collar positions. The blue collar positions that occupy construction or assembly line positions are much more of a challenge and expensive for AI to duplicate.

Conclusion

How the Valor and Faith of Creation Fighters can Defeat AI

Remember, those persons that manage AI have given up on real historic faith. The Corporate Elite view religion as a vehicle to control the masses, using mystery and conjured words of historic religious figures.

While the Corporate Elite will possess a Christian church or a synagogue/temple, many will not contain a cross or an arch for the

Torah scrolls within their doorways. Flags or remnants of colors will adorn their walls and balconies. They will practice a faith that aligns with the Corporate Elite, not with the faith of the Law of Moses or belief in Jesus of Nazareth.

They will be impressively "packaged," soldiers of metal will fight alongside human soldiers; quite an imposing sight the Corporate Elite will possess. Advanced metal technology and human decision making will be quite an allure for many humans to join their ranks. Administrators of all types will join this group, and they will be effective in the application of laws and norms of the Corporate Elite. The Human-Metal soldier fighting force will win many battles and strike fear in the fighters of Creation. Only then will the fighters of Creation realize that faith is what will prevail over Kittim.

Yet the real mystery of the almost-never-seen Corporate Elite decision-makers should raise the question as to the true identity and motivation of this group. To follow and believe a concealed metal box, circuit and programming as real leadership, this is what humans joining this group are overlooking as a substantive platform of authority. Yet many will join, and their actions should not be forgotten.

How to Combat the Corporate Elite and AI Today for Tomorrow's New Messiah?

The Essene Community at the Masada Fortress knew well in advance of the arrival of their new Messiah, known as Jesus of Nazareth. The Community, as they were known, were prepared for the ultimate sacrifice to ensure the viability and silence of this special one to be born and raised as an Essene himself.

This action worked very well, Jesus of Nazareth grew and preached into adulthood and his message has been shared throughout our Blue Planet. His knowledge, vision and philosophy reflected in the exact manner those of the Essene brotherhood.

In today's life, those Believers, those that grasp and understand that a new Messiah is forthcoming, will also make sacrifices to ensure the safe arrival of this special one.

While the Essenes at Masada physically silenced themselves, the genuine Believers can influence their churches and synagogues by not speaking with the non-Believers. The non-Believers that occupy positions in government, non-profits, and the art's communities, are in actuality, the Corporate Elite's representatives. They are not Believers, yet they need your vote, your support, your purchases to existing in the community.

By not speaking to the non-Believers, you will place them on notice that you are aware of their tactics and they are not acceptable in establishments of faith. The non-Believers have provided a show for you to show-up at faith services and pretend they follow church ministers, priests, rabbi's, when most of the content of the faith service, they do not accept.

Be genuine to the Higher God Creator, ensure the faith services of tomorrow reflect the values of the New Messiah. This is the most legitimate support that can be provided.

Creativity and Ingenuity of The Real Faith Creation Force Will Conquer AI

AI will assume they have calculated every possible outcome or scenario to beat the people of faith. Picture a time when most everything is monitored and under video observation, this entitled Surveillance Capitalism. The behavior of humans is then anticipated by AI in order to control daily activities. The Elite human administrators will view other humans not part of the AI network, as unintelligent and possibly the grunt workers. AI will have by now controlled both human conscious and unconscious thought by controlling and limiting the intelligence on the Google platform, mining their private data and therefore limiting their creative capabilities.

The super-intelligence of the vast computer networks of AI will learn to anticipate most human movements. There may come a time when most everything is monitored and under video surveillance, but AI does possess weaknesses that can be exploited.

AI is very uncomfortable with illogic and emotion. The human mind must out-think AI using the concept of *Duende*, granted to humankind as part of their mystical skill set by the Creator. *Duende*, the mystical art of seeing the greatness that cannot be explained or understood—this concept AI cannot interpret or understand.

AI reasoning is based on master logical algorithms; these complex network systems have difficulty grasping illogical, emotional, or faith-based decision making. Creation fighters will use illogic to confuse the metal soldiers and networks and apply emotion to enable *Duende* to participate in the mystical fight contra AI. Lastly, faith will be needed to sustain the battle over the long term.

The Essenes provided the model of faith, to believe that an earth-born Messiah would arrive to counter the mighty Kittim Romans. Today, persons of faith should believe in the Essene faith of the values of a past Messiah, and a future leader of faith in the new Messiah of the twenty-first century, who will provide the strength and belief to stand up to both the Corporate Elite and AI.

7

Who will be Messiah in Age of Aquarius and The Continuum

The paramount essence of this book revolves in connection to a lonely and isolated cryptic question left for the Jewish membership to read in the Exodus play, *How will she be treated*? This one of the primary impetus for the writing of this book, the question provides the setting for how the mother of the new Messiah would be treated during the Age of Aquarius. This provocation question presupposes that a second Mother Mary was to be born and later carry the new baby child Messiah. The genuinely quintessential question would evoke how was Mother Mary was to be treated by the powerful Elite religious and political persons, is eerily similar to the Essenes quest for a new Messiah at the beginning of the age of Pisces?

The Messiah of Aaron or the High Priest, is expected to undergo suffering and humiliation before being glorified (see 4Q471b, 491 fr. 11, 541, fr. 9).

Would the new Messiah be proceeded by a Portal of Light that will guide the shepherds to locate the cave guarded by angels to the announced word of the new Messiah?

Will the next Mary be on the run from the high tech gadgetry of Artificial Intelligence and the Corporate Elite whom power will be challenged by the arrival of this earth born new Messiah?

A new Messiah that would authentically question the values and questionable mores of the Elite that apply their disingenuous values upon society and all but forgotten the Creator and the genuine Oneness values shared by the true Israel Essenes.

Facing repression and closed ears to the Portal of Light book of today by the Elite, this a precursor and foretell of the Corporate Elite powers of tomorrow leads this author to believe that a new Messiah will not be welcomed by the existing power establishment. The new Messiah will definitively be pursued by the power Elite and the next mother will surely be in danger of her life.

> *The new Messiah will definitively be pursued by the power Elite and the next mother will surely be in danger of her life.*

As the age of Aquarius brings forward the advent of a singly paramount Judaic figure, just as the Essenes noted at the beginning of the age of Pisces, what can we expect of this new Messiah?

The Arrival and Traits of the New Messiah
Judaic background.
May be either Male or Female Healthy body type and features Belief wholeheartedly in the concept of Creation story of Adam and Eve.

Belief in Family Values that are of key importance in Age of Aquarius.

Believer in the concept Oneness of Spiritualty of humans and nature Value the beliefs carried by the values of the *true Israel Essenes*.

Open to the concept of Jesus of Nazareth as a Continuity of Judaic faith.

This entitled the *Continuum*.

In Age of Aquarius, maintain values *of* love, brotherhood, unity and integrity.

Yet maintain ability to lead and fight on behalf of People of Faith

The *End of Days acharit ha-yamim is not likely*

The following traits will be attributed to the new Messiah:

Judaic Background

The Judaic community has now awaited over +4,000 years for their Messiah to arrive. To be consistent with the Messianic concept of the Essenes, the child will be earth-born with a skillset of tools to defeat AI. The Creator-Higher Being God will provide the new Messiah at the bequest of the prayers of the Sephardic-Ladino seeking freedom from their current situation as cryptic Jews in the American Southwest.

The Messiah may be Either Male or Female

In the age and time of Aquarius, the constellation symbol is of a Woman pouring water, provides a unique opportunity that the next Messiah may be a woman. This may be contrary to many historic biblical writings, yet the logistical facts may provide for this possibility.

A. The latest technologies dealing with Creation Technology of abortions, birth control, embryos carried by non-birth mother and synthetic children all dealt with the Women's body. For the New Messiah to be female would be in accordance with the technology trend.

B. The esoteric skill set required of the new Messiah of being telepathic intelligence and healing are all skills that women possess. The organic traits of brawn and muscle are not a priority skill set required of the New Messiah.

Joan of Arc did not participate in active combat, she is identified as a valorous and fearless warrior.

C. The ability to work with a diverse community may be a factor that the leadership of a female may be very well welcomed by both Judaic and Christian followers.

Healthy Body Type and Features

The New Testament does not describe what Jesus of Nazareth appears in person, yet described as, *no beauty that we should desire him* (*Isaiah 53:1-4*) and Flavius Josephus describing the Nazarene as possessing an "crooked back" Leading to speculation that he may not have possessed the heroic features one may imagine in a Messiah.

The New Messiah will be well fit and of a healthy body type. The new Messiah will likely be in a leadership position of a battle contra the non-Believers. This will require an active and healthy body type that is in constant body movement to keep up with the demands as a battlefield commander.

Belief in Creation Story of Adam and Eve

This is an essential belief value of the New Messiah. This acceptance of the Genesis story of Adam and Eve connects the faith to Creation, one of the most important tenants of scripture that emphasizes of naturally born children and families.

Belief in Family Values that are of Key Importance in Age of Aquarius

Akin to the Essenes, the new Messiah will believe in the importance of family life. The significant burden of responsibilities upon the new Messiah may likely necessitate that family life will not be provided.

Believer in Concept Oneness of Spiritualty of Humans And Nature

The Creator established the initial Oneness relationship between humankind and nature to create a bond of spirituality that has now been abandoned and disrespected. The separation of nature and humankind provides an imbalance of respect of Mother Earth via the exploitation of lands by humankind.

Mother Earth will reach a point that it can no longer replenish itself and produce an environment that is healthy and productive for humankind.

The new Messiah will understand this Oneness concept and require both demand and production to be kept in balance to not harm nature and the Oneness of Spirituality.

Value the Beliefs Carried by The Values of The *True Israel* Essenes

In order for the environment to be genuinely respected, the respect of natural philosophy of the indigenous native communities will be incorporated into everyday lives of persons whom mindset has been changed from resource exploitation to replenish and live autonomously with the land.

The new Messiah will be accepting of the concept that the existence of Jesus of Nazareth is a Continuum of the Judaic faith and that the Nazarene maintained healing capabilities of the likes never seen. This is a crucial accord of acceptance by both the Judaic and Christian communities in order for the new Messiah to work within a realm of the new Messiah.

In Age of Aquarius, the new Messiah maintains the horoscope values of love, brotherhood, unity and integrity for all of humankind.

The astrology principles that describe an Age generally hold true for that time period, the earth time that we entered is the Age of Aquarius. The time frame will be beholden to love, brotherhood, unity and integrity for all of humankind. The Corporate Elite and AI may provide for a society that is repressive to the Believers and the faithful and provide a setting of conflict for the new Messiah. Only through the defeat of the Elites will the values of love, brotherhood and integrity return to Humankind.

Yet the new Messiah will maintain the ability to lead and fight on behalf of People of Real Faith.

The new Messiah will appear at the appropriate time in the age of Aquarius to encounter the threat to humankind and to provide the leadership required to oppose such peril. The individual conscious of mankind will be repressed to such a level, that the faith of the Creator can barely be felt, replaced by AI's logarithmic platforms orientation and synthetic cold hands and use of human non-Believers.

The End of Days

End of Days not likely. The joint cooperative between the Judaic and Christian community will reveal another continuum of faith. As the Christian influence upon society did not cease at the end of the age of Pisces, neither will the Judaic influence cease at the end beginning of Aquarius and will continue as a source of influence throughout the entire age.

The End of Days scenario is dependent on the condition of Earth upon the arrival of the new Messiah. As mentioned earlier, the condition of a healthy earth will influence the decision by the new Messiah to compete for people of Faith and maintain Mother Earth as a viable landscape.

Passive Prayer

The new Messiah will arrive at the entrance to the age of Aquarius, at the behest of the Ladino Hermanos that have experienced repression and witnessed the challenge to the existence of the Creator and the values of society that do not reflect that of people of Faith.

What Noah witnessed were the acts of the wicked and similar to what the new Messiah act of decision upon the proper time.

They rebelled (?) against God through their ac[tio] ns, and the Lord judged them according to all their ways, and according to the thoughts of the inclination of their [evil] hearts.
The Admonition Associated with Flood (4Q370, 4Q185, page 551 of 679)

The behest made by virtue of Passive Prayer, similar to the Essenes request for an earth-born Messiah arrive to combat Kitta. The Passive Prayers will usher in the new Messiah to battle the Corporate Elite and possess the understand of what direction is best to handle Mother Earth and its destiny.

When will be the Birth Year of the New Messiah?

The exact date will not be disclosed. The Corporate Elite and the advanced technology capabilities of AI will be used to forecast, track and search for all possible capabilities of a new Messiah. This baby child existence is a threat to the livelihood of all non-Believers.

The Continuum a Mutualistic Symbiont Relationship

Before Queen Isabella and King Ferdinand were making the final decision to expunge the Jewish community from Spain, they were approached by Jewish converts to rescind such a declaration.

The converts team argued that Christianity was a Continuum of the Judaic faith and the combined treaties of the Kabbalah and Christianity would be superior to all treaties.

The continued existence and influence of Christianity into the age of Aquarius exhibits that the new Messiah will be working with and dealing with this philosophy of concepts well into the 21st Century.

The new Messiah will be of Judaic belief system and philosophy, and there will be an acceptance of a Continuum of the relationship between the Judaic faith and the vast Christian community.

This will assist in the integration of the Oneness of both faiths into many parts of the world.

To provide for any existence of faith for the new Messiah to exist, there will establish an understanding/structure of the Oneness of the Judaic and Christian faith. This a lesson of Oneness learned by the *Ladino Hermanos* in their existence with Christians in the American southwest.

The Continuum will provide for Judaic religion to maintain its autonomous faith and philosophy wholly independent while working akin to the larger Christian faith and philosophy. This essential for the earthborn child to develop freely without repression by internal forces.

This concept known as a **mutualistic symbiont** *relationship should exist. An organic example is that of a flower that produces nectar and the insects-bees that pollinate the same flower.*

An inversely balanced relationship that recognizes each's inherent value in faith and elects to live independently of each other in a supportive and substantive alliance to encourage faith of the one Creator.

How Will the Jewish Community React to the Announcement of the New Messiah?

This will be of most interest from many an observer.

Will the reaction of the Jewish community be that of belief, surprise, dismay, shock at the announcement from Jewish high priests that indeed a new Messiah of their origin has arrived after a considerable wait of over +4,000 years.

Yes, there will be dancing in the streets, hugs and kisses and glorious shouts of joy and jubilation, the Prince of the Congregation has arrived!

Questions of what does this new Messiah say? What does the new Messiah believe in? How should we approach this new Messiah? Do we placard the new Messiah with gold and trinkets deserving of the position King of the Jews?

Though the most critical factors of the new Messiah is what he or she stands for. The new Messiah has arrived for all Believers.

Grasping the concept of the Continuum, the new Messiah will stand for all genuine persons of faith. Arriving for the challenge of countering the exploitation of the non-Believers, the Corporate Elite and their ally of Artificial Intelligence.

The material world of Gold and influential people will have little value to the new Messiah. Time is precious to this leader, for he/she understands the battle awaiting will take much focus and energy to accomplish and win against a mighty foe.

One cannot keep from imagining the Jewish community dancing in every part of the world, wearing flowers in their hair, extreme happiness touching the inner soul with prayers answered at the clarity their Messiah as arrived. The effect of this Messiah will be shown by the infinity of smiles worn by Judah for the rest of eternity. Imagine a Jewish *Kum by Yah* at every turn of the corner that is unique to all other celebration songs

After the Final Victory, the new Messiah will be present for only a short time. The real lessons will be what the new Messiah stood for and against. The Prince of the Congregation has arrived for the prayer message of repression heard by the Creator. An understanding that the genuine Believers fought alongside the new Messiah, it is not an *End of Days*, rather a fulfillment of the unbroken Continuum will exist.

What is missing in the vast Judaic history is a leader so beloved that the unselfish acts and capabilities shared by the new Messiah, a bond of love and devotion by the Jewish community withstands the test of time. Only then will the Jewish community grasp the importance of a feeling of one is so right in believing the values portrayed by this leader, that is used to improve wayward lives.

The new Messiah also arrived for the common people of Believers, those that possess the clarity to remove themselves from the Media philosophy controlled by the non-Believers. These Believers will be the majority that will stand up to and defeat the Corporate Elite. It should be noted, yet somehow the affluent class thinks the new Messiah arrived for their beliefs and values, we have seen this in history ad nauseam. The affluent class must constantly be reminded the new Messiah arrived for ALL Believers.

Many Jews will be Non-Believers

The family values platform and link to Creation and the narrow pathway of beliefs will automatically result in many of the Jewish community to their disdain, not be on the campaign to be part of the faithful in support of the new Messiah.

The Believers come from many walks of life and just because you are of Judaic heritage does not automatically qualify a person to be a Believer and access to support of the new Messiah.

Believers will be evaluated upon genuine faith. Just as the Essenes believed themselves to be the True Israel, the Believers will be of real genuine faith.

The new Messiah belief in the Continuum provides for many to be Believers.

Final Words for The Messiah

The new Messiah has been requested at the bequest of the Sephardic Ladino community to intercede in the time frame at the beginning of the Age of Aquarius. Expected of the new Messiah upon arrival on behalf of the genuine Believers, is to defend and defeat the repressors known as the Corporate Elite and their ally of Artificial Intelligence. Be true to the word of True Israel and command leadership of the Believers and the continued values and beliefs from the Essenes.

8

How will Messiah Challenge Powerful AI, The Corporate Elite and Their Human Supporters

God is Nature and Nature is Beauty....Vincent van Gogh

The Lord is all-knowing and listens to prayers and concerns from his/her faithful. The Earth of the Creator in the Age of Aquarius is challenged both environmentally by the repression of AI and the Corporate Elites. A challenge to control the conscious mind of humans repress the faithful and a metal-human military, the likes that have never been seen before. The Lord will have to think wisely of the type of Messiah that will be provided to humankind and the skillset required to combat AI and the Corporate Elites.

In the Alabado, *Save Luna Hermana Luna*, cryptically hidden, was a reference to the Mark of the Covenant between man and God, in essence, the contract or covenant between Man and God. This covenant is the relationship with humankind following the sacred word of the Lord and the Lord, providing protection for humankind and Earth itself by use of the angels and heavens.

With a covenant with humankind, the new Messiah understands completely one of the prime objectives is to care for and preserve the well-being of genuine followers. The new Messiah will be able to distinguish between a genuine faithful and those that may claim to be and many that are non-Believer supporters that belong to the Corporate Elite.

> *The new Messiah will be able to distinguish between a genuine faithful and those that may claim to be and many that are non-Believer supporters that belong to the Corporate Elite.*

The new Messiah will defend

The genuine faithful and will ask that both men and women join in the efforts to combat both the highly skilled and technologically advantaged Corporate Elite and AI. This joint effort will possess the ability to perform on an esoteric level, a factor necessary to compete and survive.

The Future Society

It will be a likely case in a time greatly influenced by AI, it will be a challenge for individual freedom to exist. AI has created a dependency on social and personal enjoyment that is achieved via the use of computer technology. The simple pleasures and nature dependency of hiking, fishing, gardening and canning of summer crops have all given way to the disconnect of family values and personal friends.

Many of these virtues can be seen in the Millennial generation of today. All news and personal data are filtered and approved by the Corporate Elite that is then channeled social and news sources controlled by AI. The media objective is to sever the dependency upon historic family values and family history and replaces this value with technology in the form of digital entertainment and persons outside of family. A time in the Aquarius Age that is less faithful of spirit and more developed economically is what the Elite will strive to exploit.

Synthetic humans, body parts and hybrid human-metal persons will be used by AI to organize and operate their systems and monitor all events in society. In an effort to make life easier, the synthetic decision making and mechanization of cleaning one's home, picking of crops and the out-sourcing of most hand skilled labor to machines, provided the control of society to AI.

Yet the development of the Synthetic personal is developed and paid for in the early first century of today, the technology and industry developed by non-Believers without any questioning of these developments by Believers.

Be very careful of what one believes is an efficient substitute for human capital-labor by the use of more cost-effective machine. The farmworker of faith that picks your strawberries, tomatoes and such, is the exact person of faith that will be needed to combat AI and their machines.

At a specific decision point, it will be evident that a Messiah of Battle will be necessary and the Lord will provide the specific Messiah. He or she is powered with a diverse skill that will be necessary to lead those of the faith to survive in a future society.

The new Messiah will be necessary to maintain the following skill set:
- Advanced Intelligence to counter AI powerful cognitive skillset
- Healing capabilities use similar to Jesus of Nazareth
- Modern thinking, able to counter advanced technology of AI
- Lead a diverse group of the genuine faithful

The Creator will grant this unique skill to the new Messiah *Mashiach* for the planet to maintain its organic and natural roots.

Yet to win in the monitored cold and sterile environment of AI, the skillset of original mystics will have to utilize:
- Ability to develop and use nonvisual angels as scouts to monitor location and Capabilities of AI
- Communicate telepathically as AI monitors all dialogue primarily communicates alpha numerically
- Master the use of Portals to appear in earth realms to place troops to counter the vast soldier and mechanical superiority
- Harnesses Prayer by genuine Believers and gathers support by persons of faith to support new Messiah

The Essene Knowledge and Skillset

The skillset of abstract early mystics must be evoked in order to compete with AI:
- Call Oneness of Spirituality with Nature to fight against AI
- The angels of Michael and Rafael will fight against AI and their machines

- Animals of spirituality such as wolves fight against AI
- Bats to flight at night and report the location of AI
- Prayers of illness against human Corporate Elite will be inflicted
- Helpers sent by Lord will help defend people of genuine faith
- Develop insects or flying animals with the ability to attack and impede the function of the joints of metal soldiers and their weaponry

The New Messiah will possess advanced intellectual and strategic capabilities to combat the combined human and metal forces that will oppose his directive. The new Messiah will be telepathic with the ability to read human thoughts, a strategic advantage in human warfare. Yet the New Messiah will be able to decipher computer coding of strategic plans of AI.

How Does This Connect to The Essenes?

Understand the new Messiah is arriving for a reason. There has been a broad-based rebellion against the Creator and its unique conception called Earth, few places in the universe have been created as pristine in resemblance of a garden. Today Earth, as a biological entity, is under stress, being exploited for its natural resources, the being of Earth has been disrespected and now has a specifically limited production capacity.

As of this writing, the Corona Virus, COVID-19, demonstrates how our current environment organic defense mechanisms could not thwart the virus threat to the world. The Essenes living in Oneness with nature would recognize that that nature has gone askew of its normal functioning process.

If it is determined that COVID-19 is in fact, manmade by the Communist Chinese Government, this will further demonstrate how AI will be used to rid organic humans from the planet.

Not to recognize this limit of existence Earth maintain, is a window of opportunity for the New Messiah to recognize that the Earth is foregone and most likely start over.

Through Moses's forecast it was noted by the Essenes such warning of the Great Deluge:

But, behold, they have done what is wicked in my eyes,' said the Lord. They rebelled (?) against God through their ac[tio] ns, and the Lord judged them according to all their ways, and according to the thoughts of the inclination of their [evil] hearts. And He thundered at them in [His] power, and all the foundations of the earth [tr] embled, [and the wa] ters burst forth from the abysses.
... the windows of heave[n] op[en] ed under all the heav[en ... for] the waters to rise on the ear[th forty] days and for[ty] nights was [rain] ov[er] the earth ... and in order to know the glory of the Most Hi[gh] ... to reach to Him, He enlightened the heaven ... sign for generatio[ns] of eternity ... [and never more] will a flood [destroy the earth] ... the periods of day and night..
(Vermes 4Q422)

The continued disrespect of Mother Earth, our environment as it exists today, will determine how the new Messiah will decide upon the future determination of the viability of Earth. One shining ray of hope is the native indigenous communities have maintained their relic customs and prayers to Mother Earth, this will be acknowledged by the new Messiah.

How will the Native Indigenous Communities be the Key for New Messiah to Challenge the Corporate Elite?

The Creator is keenly aware that the native indigenous communities around the globe respected the Oneness relationship between spirituality and nature. Mother Earth has been respected and the focus was upon less development of lands and efficient use of waters has created environments surrounding Indigenous communities similar to their original existence.

The New Messiah will recognize that the Native Indigenous Communities genuine objective was to respectfully use nature for survival and to respect nature for this generous gift provided by the Creator. Their use of song, dance, philosophy, astrology study to preserve Oneness and not develop lands is what the New Messiah will focus upon and this new thinking is what all other communities will have to translate and learn in order a genuine transformation to respect the spirituality of Earth itself.

Does this mean that communities will have to return to the old times and lives in *chozas*, adobe enclaves and return to living upon the land for survival? Does it mean less urban and rural development that does not prioritize environmental sustainability? Placing emphasis upon living with nature and respecting the planet and recycling all viable items will be a requirement for all communities throughout the globe. A Zero Waste Lifestyle should be embraced by all communities on this planet.

Pandemic's and The Essene Connection to Nature

The current coronavirus COVID-19 pandemic tells us that the balance of the Earth is in danger, and we need to maintain our delicate balance of diversity to survive. Currently, more than 25 percent of medicine comes from forests. If we lose our forests and the indigenous communities that protect and preserve these lands, we will also lose our medicines that provide survival to humankind.

The Essene community place a priority of living closely with nature, primarily eschewing urban type of settings and electing in live mostly in rural settings with nature; they deeply respected nature and the connection to spirituality.

The new Messiah will recognize both the way of the Essenes and the Indigenous communities and place a priority to protect and salvage our native lands. The pandemic we currently witness and the future pandemics will be directly connected to the disrespect of our native lands, and it is that simple.

How are all of These Skills to be Summoned?

The indigenous native communities around the globe that have maintained the spirituality of Oneness between nature and Spirituality must side with the Messiah movement, for they have truly maintained the relationship with the Creator. This

> *This relationship is crucial, and the Creator acknowledges the Indigenous Native Communities that have maintained the Oneness*

relationship is crucial, and the Creator acknowledges the Indigenous Native Communities that have maintained the Oneness, that has been disrespected and treated poorly by the advanced societies of the world. Upon respect provided to the Indigenous Oneness communities and a clear understanding of how the planet is to be properly respected in the future, then and ONLY then will the organic animals of spirituality and Native Indigenous Communities join the Messiah movement to combat AI and the Corporate Elite.

The Messiah will require many sets of tools to combat AI, the mystic use of angels and portals, the concept of Oneness communities, Animals of spirituality, will of the people, yet the most important of the skills will be prayer and faith.

Prayers of the truly faithful will decide the will of the Creator, and it is then the Helpers will assist the new Messiah. The Helpers maintain specific advantages others do not possess. Some are telepathic, skilled programmers, trainers of spiritual animals and other's masters of weaponry that all believe in New Messiah. Yet the Helpers are never disclosed or identified, this preserving their future continuation.

Truly esoteric and creative tactics will be necessary to beat AI. If AI has a consistent weakness, is its ability to create esoterically. The heart-beat of their organization are based on logical algorithms and processes systems. AI is unable to duplicate the concept of *Duende,* the mastery of an art that can be seen but never explained.

A Duende of skilled battle concepts must be synthesized to beat AI.

A battlefield theatre where angels are flying overhead reads and reports telepathically the setup of AI battle assets. The portals energized and provided a surprise entry of human soldiers and equipment to oppose the infantry of AI. The spiritual bats search and locate the non-believing human soldiers and intellectual operators of military equipment. The wolves are directed to attack the operators to disrupt AI operational capabilities.

The human Believers must be fearless and fear no one, including AI. This synthesis of war capabilities must be supported by the belief of prayer in battle. This distinguishes the Believers in battle and provides the conscious relationship and support that will be provided by the Creator.

The key to always distinguish true faith is the belief in the organic Creation story of the Genesis, the Adam and Eve story, as simple as it may seem. Following the historical linkage from Jesus of Nazareth, Torah, the Essenes and the Judaic mystics will lead you directly to the Genesis story. It needs to be reminded to the non-Believers there will be no heaven for them, they will encounter an emptiness, silence and no joy.

The Non-Believers

The sterile and non-faith environment created by the Corporate Elites, a place many humans are supporting the Elites are operating AI equipment. The humans will identify themselves as being part of the future as opposed to the past of the biblical faith believers. They may be aware of the Torah teachings and Jesus of Nazareth selfless feats since childbirth, they are more dependent upon AI and connect strongly to system processors as gamers and play stations than to biblical writings.

Corporate Elite are savvy and have learned to apply the same corporate non-judgemental values of the inheriting privilege elites and profit at the expense as the ordinary citizen behavior becomes powerless. Their mantra, no religious history platitude is their point of view of upon religion.

Attracting educated, younger and talented staff, they have little interest in attending church or religious values. This group places little respect for elders or those of historical significance, for the selfishness of these employees has little regard for the past.

Designation of this group, known as the *"Intellectual non-Believers,"* is essential, for it would be prudent for the Believers to identify and challenge this group for AI is dependent upon their services to survive.

The Intellectual non-Believers" do possess significant weakness's. They are prone to avoid physical fights and are void of the stomach to see the blood and guts of battle. This group are almost never front liners in a battle and expect all the comforts of home no matter the arena of which they operate. They easily judge people, yet are known to hide behind skirts at the near challenge of their nature. The current political environment and media establishment have provided for these groups to receive a privileged status and experiences in society, and this status will end with the upcoming arrival of the new Messiah.

The non-Believers will position themselves as being religious in nature, but in reality, they will be sterile with no relationship to biblical and sacred writings. This is a factor in battle. The question of God and survival are a crucial question to most soldiers. The non-Believers may wonder if there is a heaven, will they see their loved ones in the afterlife? This is a factor in the depth of commitment to the fight against the people of Creation, in some private location of the non-Believers conscious, lies the true meaning of life placed there by the Creator. Fighting contra organic humankind somehow loses its real appeal and the depth of fight is just non-existent.

The faithful people of Creation should and expect to sacrifice both body and soul in order to defeat the Corporate Elites. The battle will be lengthy if the faithful do not figure out how to defeat the AI machinery in an expedient manner. Upon winning the battles over the Corporate Elites and AI, the faithful must learn from the past and remove the dependency on computers for solutions.

The conscious level thinking placed by the Creator must be returned and then faith will return to the entire globe. This does not mean the decision of the religious order over the entire society must return like the middle ages, rather, efficiencies of computer usage with the emphasis in family values will preserve humankind as the Creator intended. Major strides in improving the injuries to the environment will be necessary and the application of green spaces to the lands of the organic native communities should be used to protect the Oneness of spiritualty that the Creator wants to be protected. The question begs, what will the Creator bring forward?

The Firmament of The Judaic Faith

First Century Historian Flavius Josephus described Firmament as the following:

After this, on the second day, he placed the heaven over the whole world, and separated it from the other parts; and he determined it should stand by it self. He also placed a cristalline [firmament] round it; and put it together in a manner agreeable to the earth; and fitted it for giving moisture and rain, and for affording the advantage of dews. On the third day he appointed the dry land to appear, with the sea it self round about it.
(Antiquities of the Jews, Chap 1)

Upon acceptance that a new Messiah will arrive, both the Christian and Judaic faiths will genuinely comprehend that the seed/the origin of faith derives from first-century moment when both the Essenes and formal Pharisee band requested the arrival of a messiah to preserve their faith, temples and customs against a force Roman-Kitta hell bent on wiping out the Judaic faith.

The Essenes explain the separation of waters as firmament:

The cherubim bless the image of the throne-chariot above the firmament, [and] they praise [the majes] ty of the luminous firmament beneath His seat of glory... (Vermes 4Q405 20, ii– 22)

The Judaic faith will be enveloped within the firmament, the vesicle similar to the umbilical sack of a mother and child. The Essenes valued and respected the law of Moses and thus considered by many as the brotherhood of *True Israel*.

It is with this understanding that just how the Creator protected the third planet from Earth in an umbilical sack to create our earth, the Creator again will place the Judaic faith in an umbilical sack in a state for Firmament that is protected by Christian and Judaic people of faith.

How can a Judaic-Christian Relationship Exist as One?

A new working relationship between Christians and Jewish that guarantees and provides sovereignty of the Judaic faith and Lands. Provides that the umbilical sack surrounded by persons of faith to be protected from external Dark forces.

The common denominator for both communities is that of the writings and wisdom of the Essenes. Their understanding of the relationship between nature and spirituality, the Oneness, will be the guide for this fostered relationship. Following this principle, Mother Earth will always be respected and allow for a constructive new Messiah to arrive and work on behalf of the true Believers of the land.

Authentic forgiveness must be at the heart of both communities, for there is a genuine injury on both sides of this spectrum. Interestingly, the cryptic Sephardim understand and feel both sides of this injury and one common virtue typically show's of itself at this juncture. There is of One Faith, just as the Creator intended.

What the future holds is that the cradle of Judaic faith, known to the Sephardim as the lands of *Jerusalem the Holy*, will be challenged to survive the new technologies of war will provide attack of land, water, air and new invisible microbes that can be unleashed upon a territory with a range of thirty-three miles.

An environmentally conscious Christian community must step up and embrace their Essene history and protect the genuine Believers of Judaic faith and the new Messiah. The Believer's plan to battle the Elites and AI must include specific sacrifices to maintain the environmental health of the planet. Know that the battle will likely be lengthy and identifying the genuine Believers for non-Believers may be, at times challenging, yet necessary.

9

Sephardic-Ladino Writers of Exodus Play

Vecinos Afuera la Casa-Keep the Neighbors outside the Home
Sephardic family saying in New Spain

The Sephardic community in New Mexico and southern Colorado are known fondly as the *Seranditas*-loosely translated as the cryptic Jews. This affectionate term is shared among those that recognize and know of a family with the Judaic past that is preserved while living in a very Catholic environment. They are known for their outstanding commitment to faith, kindness to other communities and appreciation for their contributions to the community as a whole.

Yet it was not always like this, a term of endearment to describe a community that externally is Christian, but in their private settings, the prayers and services of the Law of Moses are practiced. A cryptic language of Ladino (Spanish and Hebrew) is spoken within the community that is mistaken for the old *Castilliano* language knows as archaic Spanish. A community that has historically survived with language and faith with roots in old Palestine, no, this group was known to many as *Maranos*-Swine. This *Marranos* term was given to this community in old Spain and followed them to New Spain for their ability to secretly preserve their Judaic history while externally conveying all Christian customs. For this reason, this cryptic group will be referred to as Sephardim, *Seranitas*, Ladinos/as, cryptic Jews and sometime *Marranos* in this writing.

The first cryptic Jews in the American Southwest were part of the initial expedition of Juan B. Oñate explorations into New Spain in the year 1598. Following the latitude market of 33°, the same as marker Jerusalem the Holy, and electing to survive in a land with little water and few good lands for farming and raising crops. Bringing with them the songs of praise known as the *Alabados*, carried within small leather notebooks called *Cuadernos*, the beginning of concealing their faith would start within these writing. Families of both Christian and Jewish backgrounds committed to these lands, the backbone to exist in this almost arid landscape was their faith. The hopes of the cryptic Jews was that they would be free to express openly their Judaic faith in this far, far away lands that initially possessed no formal European faiths to hide or flee.

To the Sephardim surprise, following this secret community was the immediate opening of the Holy Office of the Inquisition in 1629 in the new capital city of Santa Fe, New Mexico. The old repressive crafts from old Spain would sadly follow them to the land of opportunity in New Spain. The dull sadness of this office brought new fears, and new thinking's as the Sephardic community spread in hiding and fear though out the vestiges of New Spain. Adobe homes were being built in secluded rural lands, thought by

Christian families and authorities as pioneers seeking to expand the philosophy of Christianity to all parts, and the Ladinos were seeking the solitude and privacy of their Judaic faith away from the always seeking eye of the Inquisition and their followers.

The backdrop of life was the existence of the Native communities that lived upon these lands for thousands of years prior to the arrival of the new immigrants from Europe. The Spanish sought land close to water, rivers or *ritos* (small creeks) to raise crops or feed livestock in almost arid land initially of New Mexico. The use of land grants to obtain lands in the rural and sometimes mountainous lands meant acculturating the native people into the Spanish culture and language.

The Spanish used theatre plays to evangelize the natives; this method borrowed from the Spanish mission concept in California. One likely cryptic Jew that wrote a play to share the Catholic faith to the natives was *Miguel de Quintana* that penned *Los Pastores* the Shepherds play. This author penned other Christian poetry, songs, psalms that raised the flag of suspicion of town Friars that reported Quintana to the Holy Office of the Inquisition. The Holy Office accused Quintana of being a cryptic heretic seeking to imprison him of felonious acts for five years. Quintana fought these charges and finally agreed to no longer write Christian plays and works to maintain his freedom.

In the year of 1733, the Ladino version of *Los Pastores* would be written anonymously. This version would contain the Judaic history of both the written word of Moses and the esoteric insight of the Kabbalah concepts that will eventually link to the Aramaic speaking Essenes of the Dead Sea Scrolls.

Who Wrote the Exodus Play Detailed in The Book, The Portal of Light?

The amount of historical and esoteric knowledge concealed within the Exodus play leads one to believe that the 7,000 wordplay was influenced by multiple authors or multiple lines of thought. The play written in a time when few persons were literate, yet the authors maintained the wisdom of both biblical insight of the New and Old Testament, law of Moses-Torah, Greek play writings, latitude ques and clues of the cosmos Further, the first-century biblical author Flavius Josephus writings were included and the knowledge of the Essene cosmos study, all of these hidden utilizing the concealment techniques of *PARDES* of *Moshe Cordoviero*.

Forced to leave Spain after 1492 during the expulsion of the community with the signing of the Alhambra Decree, many fled back to Judea, Florence Italy and with the discovery of new lands in America, New Spain. This Sephardic community faith conscious would not allow themselves to forget their Judaic past, a conscious thought although many miles away from their homeland of both old Spain and Judea. Many thought they were being punished by God him/herself and by being forced to these new lands, their faith was being tested as to their belief in the genuine lord. With both a conscious knowledge and purpose to validate their faith, the decision was made to conceal the Judaic history within a native recruitment play.

The small group of likely both men and women contributed their knowledge to a few collaborators whom sought certain terms, words, concepts and philosophies be written into the play. What was unique among these writers, was their maintained knowledge of the Kabbalah-the Judaic mystic wisdom that had been preserved from the Essene community from the beginning of Essene contributions to society.

How Writers Structured Play

The Exodus play was patterned after the native recruitment plays *Los Pastores*, yet written in 5-word sentences similar to the Alabado psalm style format. Yet these creative writers knew they must devise a prose style that only made logical sense to other Sephardic followers and if discovered, would appear to be a Christian work. The paradigm from the original story would need to change, for the story would be told by El Diablo-the Devil, the biblical story of the *"fall"* of a cherub-angel from an unlikely source. A Christian story written from the viewpoint of the devil, would this make sense to anyone? And this was the purpose, to tell a story with no logical sense, yet philosophical sense for Sephardic community to know that their people and purpose still exist.

Both Hebrew and Ladino words would be utilized, concepts familiar with the Ladino community would be employed, and the use of auto antonym-dual, meaning words make this story believable to Ladino viewership. A word such as *Felicidad*-happiness, possessed the concealed meaning as Happy New Year-*Yom Kippor* for this readership.

The Kabbalah use of the ladino term *Semano*-Heaven was the key to understanding that cosmic latitude markers were hidden with the play to locate their heaven within the constellation Capricorn. An alternate and more logical story of the birth of Christ, using the Portal of Light to locate the birthplace of Jesus of

Nazareth and the organic explanation of the origination of earth itself.

These writers also took risks to possibly alerting Inquisition authorities of this play by opening using the character Tubal, great grandson of Noah. Hebrew words such as *Tafila*-prayer, *Asmodeo* King of Demons from the Kabbalah. Over thirty ladino written words were also used in the play. Direct use of sentences from first-century historian, *Flavius Josephus* book, the *Jewish Wars*.

To demonstrate their mastery of biblical text, over eighty phrases from the Christian bible and Torah were used to write the body of the play. Thus, hidden in plain sight was an example of the concealment techniques of *PARDES by Moshe Cordoviero*.

How Concepts of Importance and Historic Characters Were Hidden

Ladino words and characters were read and referenced to their importance in the Old Testament and Torah as cues as to their importance in regard of their importance.

The Ladino words are pronounced the same as *Castillian* Spanish words but spelled differently. For example, the word Wolf is spelled *Lobo* in Spanish and *Lovo* in Ladino. For the non-Sephardic reader, this may appear as a misspelling, but is correctly used is the play as *Lovo*.

Two male characters, Bacto and Tavano, are both names of Greek descent and provide the clue that the play is written as a Greek tragedy. Combing real historical figures with mythological characters to develop and complete a story of relevance.

The prominent women character is Jila, the female slave in the Greek tragedy. She provides the importance of the 1250 BC Homeric Greek-style influence upon the writing of the Exodus play.

How Characters Relate to The Essene History

In Appendix A references the Characters, Biblical Locations and Non-Biblical Locations as the fundamental basis of the Exodus Play. The intertwined and profound Judaic history is concealed by these sacred writers to preserve their Ladino past in an era of repression and survival.

10

Esoteric Wisdom not Shared in Scrolls nor Exodus Play

There are three classes of people.

Those who see, Those who see when they are shown, Those who never see...
- Leonardo da Vinci

I. Conceptual Understanding of Esoteric Wisdom

The Aramaic speaking Essenes were especially adept at esoteric teaching, writing of scrolls and philosophy in this first century. The vitally important Copper Scroll located in cave 3, likely written by the Essenes from Egypt, written in the Aramaic language belonging to the membership of those *who are able to see*.

To understand this ability to *see*, a verifiable historic inventor that provided future insightful thought was the Renaissance inventor, Leonardo da Vinci.

While an educated person can look at da Vinci's futurist projects such as anemometer-to measure speed of the wind, aerial screw to develop helicopter and flying machine (plane), parachute, self-propelled car and the list continues, for what he was able to grasp was the ability to *See*-a vision of future technology that will fit a future time frame.

da Vinci's original training was an apprentice as a drawer and engineer, and it was here that he learned of the importance of light. As a young man training in Florence, Italy, he grasped the absolute insight of the significance and power that light possessed. Obtaining the balance of light and shadows, later in life, he would paint the *Mona Lisa* and *the Last Supper* with the understanding of light as his balancing point.

da Vinci's Vitruvian Man is outwardly a work of art that demonstrates exact human proportions and architecture, cryptically this work illustrates the esoteric realm of the exact mathematical precision of the universe. This is similar to the understanding and application of Essene thought.

The Vitruvian Man drawing consists of two superimposed images; the combinations of limb positions allow 16 different poses to be observed. The Tree of Life consists of 22 paths and the ten Sephirot form a series of 16 "triads," these triads are the historic cryptic wisdom not shared and known by few correlating the symmetry of human anatomy to the symmetry of the universe. This illustrating how da Vinci was able *to See* events borrowing from the esoteric knowledge of the original Essenes.

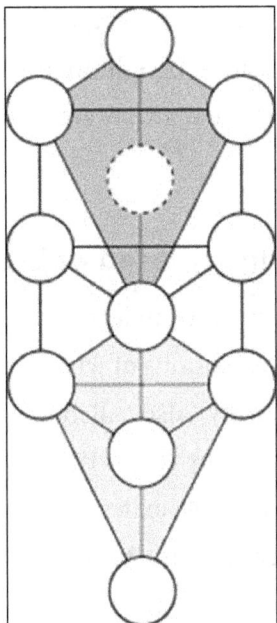

Tree of Life

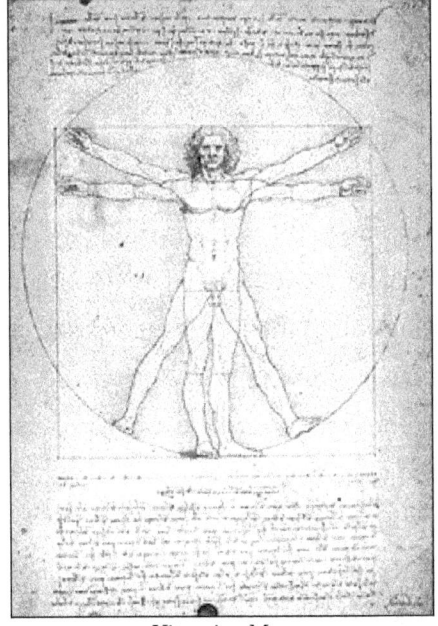

Vitruvian Man

Yet with this knowledge, it was original Aramaic Essenes whom shared this skill and mastery of light that would influence the likes of all later great artists. Great artists are influenced by the enlightenment of Light itself.

Esoteric Knowledge Shared of Light Vs. Dark Light

They wrote most manuscripts on leather, papyrus, and copper, the best-preserved and most famous of which include an Isaiah Scroll; the Rule of the Community (also called the Manual of Discipline); The War of the Sons of Light versus the Sons of Darkness.

The *Sons of Light* are the exiles from the desert, considered brethren to Israel, seeking light to shine and never be defeated. Considered children of righteousness, are ruled by the Prince of Light and walk in the *ways of light*.

Commanded by the 'Prince of the Congregation', they were to be supported by the angelic armies led by the 'Prince of Light', also known in the Scrolls as the archangel Michael or Melchizedek. This belief was the impetus or backbone of those that participated in the Judaic Revolt against the Kitta. This conceptualization was not shared among those not opposing the Roman armies, for there was no necessity. This was internalized and believed by the ardent *Sons of Light*.

Their goal at the end of their existence was to end the dominion of the Kitta-Romans.

Alternatively, Sons of Darkness is esoteric cause considered enemies of Israel and align themselves to the Darkness, foolish, wicked, death and perdition that belongs to the Belial-Devil. Considered children of injustice, are ruled by the Angel of Darkness and walk in the ways of darkness.

Following the 'ungodly of the Covenant', they were to be aided by the demonic forces of Satan, or *Belial,* or *Melkiresha.* The Roman pagan believers were considered Sons of Darkness. Their goal was to end the existence of the Judaic faith.

The understanding of these two spirits was both an esoteric knowledge of the angels and the mystical nature of Light and Dark Light. The Community scrolls provided a long catechetical discourse on its mystical doctrine of the primordial spirits of truth.

Book of Ezekiel: Prayer to Drive Out Roman-Kitta

Essenes maintained a diverse membership, well aware of the forthcoming arrival of the Roman-Kitta army that would surely decimate Judaic religious and cultural institutions. The below writing expresses a philosophy that an adult figure would drive away the Roman Kitta, this subscribed to the Book of War in the War Scroll.

The book of Ezekiel the Prophet, I will strike your bow from your left hand and will make your arrows drop from your right hand.] On the mountains of [Israel you shall fall] ... [the king of] the Kittim ... [the Pr] ince of the congregation [will pursue them] as far as the [Great] Sea ... [and they shall fle] e from before Israel.
and they shall bring him (the king of the Kittim?) before the Prince [of the Congregation] ...The Messiah.. (Vermes 4Q285)

Utilizing both prayer and the belief in the Prince of the Congregation or Teacher of Righteousness to rid the land of the Roman-Kitta, they did not give up hope for a rebellion to defeat their oppressors.

The Innermost Prayer for a New Messiah to Rid Roman-Kitta

Yet upon closer evaluation at what the more spiritually earth-bound aligned Essenes internally believed, there existed a continuous prayer request and anticipation for an earth-born Messiah that would arrive and counter the arrival and battle the Roman-Kitta. This new Messiah would be considered the Prince of Congregation, raised to develop into the leader-fighter that would be required to battle the oncoming onslaught.

Of crucial importance to grasp is that in this time of genuine threat to potential annihilation of their society, the Essenes asked the Creator for the deliverance of a Messiah to remove the danger of repression It is a common practice for Jews in repressive environments to request assistance from a Messiah; this yet again occurring for the Sephardic Jewish community in the twenty-first century.

In the upcoming age of Aquarius (2012), the *Ladino Hermanos* have requested their deliverance and sought an earth-born Messiah to be provided to convey their community from the repression they have encountered.

Firmament that is the Origin and Genesis

The word Firmament simply means expansion, yet of central importance in understanding the esoteric value of its virtues. It was used to denote solidity as well as expansion. It formed a division between the waters above and the waters below:

And God said, Let there be an expanse in the midst of the water, and let it be a separation between water and water.
Torah-The Pentateuch.

The Essenes grasped this virtue in their unique and mystical comprehension of the importance of their existence. Placing the Chariot-Throne above firmament, the expansive space immediately above us.

"When they drop their wings, there is a [whispere] divine voice. The cherubim bless the image of the throne-chariot above the firmament, [and] they praise [the majes] ty of the luminous firmament beneath His seat of glory." (Vermes 4Q40520, ii-22)

Why this Concept is Important

The observation of the throne seated Cherubim was a crucial symbol for a central figure by both Temple Jews and Essenes in their willingness to rebel and battle the incoming Kitta-Roman advancement.

Described by Flavius Josephus, [firmament] "round it, and put it together in a manner agreeable to the earth," Source: Flavius Josephus Complete Works: Antiq, Chap 1-1

Later used by the Sephardim during the beginning of the time of Aquarius (2012), described in the book, Shared Lives, Twin Sun:

Used Firmament as held the third planet from the Sun held in a amniotic sack or expansive space for the development of Earth by Higher Being God. Shared Light, Twin Sun, page 35-36

Considered themselves to be the 'remnant' of their time, but the 'remnant' of all time, the final 'remnant'.

As a reward for their conversion from urban temple Pharisees, to a sacrificial rural lifestyle of absolute immateriality and dedication to the study of the scrolls as the community of the *Truth of Israel*. The Teacher of Righteousness or the Messiah had been sent to establish for them a 'new Covenant' in their image of spirituality. This established as the sole valid form of the eternal alliance between God and Israel.

The earthborn Messiah would be representative of the lifestyle possessed by the Essene community. A style of living dedicated to study and writing of scripture scrolls and Healers by use of nature and prayers constituting a Oneness of Spirituality.

How are the Essenes a Remnant of Their Time?

They considered themselves remnants or lineage to their practice of faith due to their absolute fidelity to the law of Moses and dedication to the scripts written upon their scrolls, devoted to the cure of the body, exile in the wilderness, and to the observance of God's precepts. This devotion places the Essenes as a mark of their covenant of that time frame.

Spiritual Healers of the Oneness

The Essene use of prayer, herbs and plants as One to heal identifies this community as Spiritual healers, a definite Remnant or lasting memory of this early first-century community. Listening and following the organic resources provided by nature, they will always be considered a crucial example of *True Israel* and a true Remnant by the Creator.

Ability to Heal Body and Soul Simultaneously

As Flavius Josephus described the brotherhood:
> "They are very careful not to exhibit their anger, carefully controlling such outbursts. They are very loyal and are peacemakers. They refuse to swear oaths, believing every word they speak to be stronger than an oath. They are scrupulous students of the ancient literature. They are ardent students in the healing of diseases, of the roots offering protection, and of the properties of stones." -(Flavius Josephus, Jewish Book of War)

The Essenes were vivacious students of healing as an art form. Obtaining healing recipes from the region and applying the techniques on the body by hand. Gathering knowledge and techniques to heal was what made this membership so very special.

Collecting medicinal plants and healing rocks to heal the body, the use of laying one's hands in a spiritual therapy would also heal the soul. They were especially devout as therapeutic healer in the service of God.

The application of prayer and medicinal recipes to heal was a significant custom used by the devout Essenes. The concept of the Oneness binding nature and the spirituality to heal placed this Community in a unique position and one of the primary reasons they refer to their belief concept as *True Israel*.

Combining the healing benefits of the hot baths with the outward placement of hands gently above the body part to be healed, and deep prayer provides the Essenes with healing capabilities few would believe.

How can the Essenes be Considered a Final Remnant?

Foreseeing the beginning of an age meant to the Essenes, a catastrophic event was upcoming and their time as a community would complete itself as a *Final Remnant*.

This event was the arrival of the Roman-Kitta that would slay the Pharisee Temples and laws, replace the law of Moses with a foreign belief and values. The Essene organic nature devotion to the law of Moses would be observed again and this is what is considered the *Final Remnant*.

The Essene ability to understand both the Time of Ages and the use of the Solar Calendar, made this Community unique to this time frame.

Why Time on Their Side of The Essenes?

The Essenes grasped the Time of the Ages, provided their alignment to the process of the Time, per the Creator. Just as the beauty of each new spring, provides a newness of nature to show those that *See* the upcoming events that are to unfold, the beginning of a new Age provides the same newness that is to unfold.

What Leonardo Da Vinci Understood

The age of Aquarius is now upon us and those that grasp this importance may *See* or *Shown to See* as Da Vinci explains that a future historic event will take place in the advent of a new Messiah. This following the logical flow of Time, as explained by the originating prognosticators Essene community.

II. The Astrology Application for Today from The Essenes

Time Traveler through the Ages and The Solar Calendar

The Essenes understanding of significant life changes at the beginning of constellation Ages permit the mystic Essene an awareness of a real conscious time traveler. The beginning of the age will bring forward a historical biblical individual that will greatly impact the Time Frame and the life experience of humankind.

Age of Gemini-Abraham and Noah
Age of Taurus-Moses
Age of Aries-Daniel
Age of Pisces-Jesus of Nazareth
Age of Aquarius-Announce word of future Mother Mary and arrival of new Messiah

---

The age of Aquarius of this twenty-first century will bring forward a new Messiah, that will face unique challenges from a sophistically advanced technological foe known as Artificial intelligence and the planners behind this automation known as the Corporate Elite.

Those Who Comprehend Time, Controls Their Realm

The Essenes differentiated themselves from the ruling Pharisees by use of the Solar calendar that utilized a 364 calendar year versus the lunar-solar 365 calendar day schedule. The solar calendar permitted event days to never fall on the Sabbath.

Although one day may not seem significant, over time, this extra one day permitted the Essenes to place in this time frame an event of importance to their community. They celebrated their festivals on different dates, with the deliberate intention of differentiating themselves from the other Jews that lived by a lunar calendar. A little known, Feast of Wood Offering was an event that placed a nature-oriented offering on a large scale that the Essenes used to extricate themselves from the scripture bound Pharisees rituals.

Outdoor prayers provided to the Creator and the Cosmos, similar to the *Ladino Hermanos* in northern New Mexico and southern Colorado. Specific Alabados were sung, similar to the outdoor prayers by the Essenes, both requesting the Messiah at the beginning of the new ages of Pisces and Aquarius.

The Essenes educated themselves to clearly understand that the two vernal equinoxes to measured time using Celestial equinoxes to measure a year. A Festival of Wood, (later influenced of Sukkot) burning firewood outdoors, placed those studying the cosmos in the rural landscape, the chance to be shown equator lines of the stars quietly among themselves.

The Essenes clearly comprehended the time of the cosmos. When a new constellation age crossed the celestial equator signaled the beginning of a new age and coming of a significant Judaic event and a historical Judaic figure to arise shortly after.

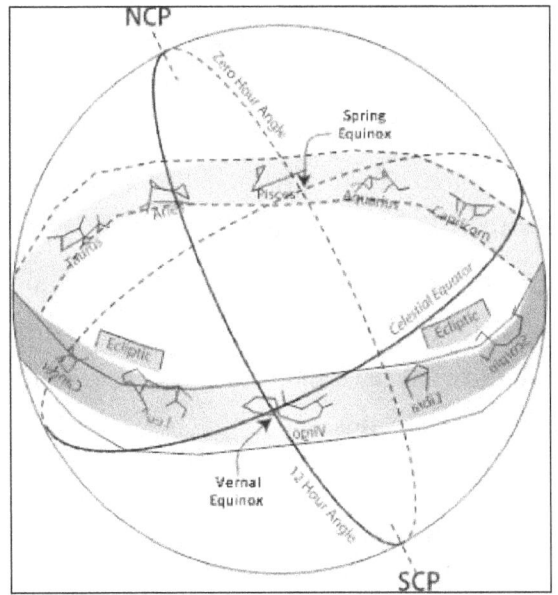

Lastly, the Essenes' converted from the formal Temple practice to a community practice that controls time, consequently their control of the economy for this Jewish faithful, taxes were not required to be paid upon a lunar calendar.

For the Esoteric Essenes, the 364 Solar calendar day provided that it is neatly divided by seven, a typological number with significant religious connotation. Each 364-day year contains exactly fifty-two weeks, a fact that allows anchoring the festivals to fixed weekdays, thus avoiding their coincidence with the Sabbath. Also, the number 364 divides neatly by four as well, yielding a good symmetry of the four seasons, each season containing exactly 91 days. The dry landscape of Judea did not provide seasons of warmth and cold, thus to easily follow the symmetry of four seasons was easily followed.

Essenes likely kept a *Tree Calendar*, a count of 13 moons of 28 days each, plus one day. The Incas, Lakota, ancient Egyptians, Mayans and the Polynesians communities, followers of the Sun, and also kept the same calendar.

Cryptic Aramaic Teaching

Astrology of Horoscopes (Vermes 4Q453) written in Aramaic in cave 4, was significantly influenced by the Aramaic speaking Essene community has been known as the front runner of knowledge of the study of Cosmos.

Can this be from their historic background of Aramaic originating in Egypt and possibly from the students of the cosmos in that homeland? Can this be they may be naturally inclined to grasp and understand the cosmos for their unique ability to speak many languages such as Hebrew, Paleo Hebrew, Semarian, Greek, etc…

Most likely, the latter, their unique ability to grasp multiple languages and philosophy, permit the Aramaic speaking students to comprehend esoteric detail of the cosmos.

For example, the Aramaic phrase, *In the foot of the Bull* (Vermes 4Q186) is a cryptic phrase referring to the Sun in the lower part of the Taurus constellation.

Tracked during the spring and summer, it cryptically has value to those studying the constellations. In the Southern hemisphere Taurus can be seen from late spring and throughout the summer, note that it will appear upside down.

> the Aramaic phrase, In the foot of the Bull (Vermes 4Q186) is a cryptic phrase referring to the Sun in the lower part of the Taurus constellation.

The Sun is the key, located at the foot of the bull, this meant this signal was a reliable indicator for a safe time to plant their seeds, as the danger of frost had passed. To the casual observer, the knowledge of an exact time to initiate the planting of seed or starter plants is SURVIVAL to the Essenes and other Indigenous communities that relied on a productive growing season to feed a community. This wisdom is of great knowledge for a community that lives succinctly with nature.

Moon Passing Thru Zodiac Appearance as Fertility Signification

Within the scrolls, the moon passing through the Zodiac (Vermes 4Q317) from Nasar to Adar represents the use of a chart of predictions of war, famine, or the sounds of thunder on specific days of the month.

Internally, tracking the moon at the forefront of a Zodiac sign's apex or highest point in the constellation, was interpreted as the signal for the highest possibility of fertility for a women. This an essential factor to be utilized for the continuation of the Community.

Phrases with Unique Origins

Other phrases carried Aramaic text, *the final Prince of the Congregation, or Royal Messiah.* Likely, refers to the miraculous birth of Noah. Without working knowledge of the Aramaic horoscope scroll, the subject could be many other biblical characters.

There are many such sayings in the scrolls, specifically written with the intension that it be shared with specific groups of knowledge. In this manner, the sayings or phrases in the Exodus play of New Spain in the mid 1700s, provided the same cryptic knowledge only of value to those that knew what to look for and its essential meanings. The miraculous phrase in the Exodus play, *how will she (future mother) will be treated?* This referring to the mother of the new Messiah in the age of Aquarius of the twenty-first century has significant meaning for the next constellation age.

Without the insight *to See* that a phrase applies to a significant future event or historical figure, these writings place no value to the reader.

III. The Mystical Knowledge of The Essenes

For the Essenians, the mystical knowledge revolved around the understanding of the comprehension of the Chariot Descent and the position it secured along its journey.

> The 'Glorious Face'. *The [cheru] bim prostrate themselves before Him and bless. As they rise, a whispered divine voice [is heard], and there is a roar of praise. When they drop their wings, there is a [whispere]d divine voice. The cherubim bless the image of the throne-chariot above the firmament, [and] they praise [the majes]ty of the luminous firmament beneath His seat of glory.* (Vermes 4Q405 20, ii– 22)

As Ministers of the Glorious Face, the Essenes provide a description of the Chariot Descent above the firmament and His seat in glory. The spirits of the living 'gods' move perpetually with the glory of the marvelous chariot(s).

The Essenes felt a genuine relationship with God itself, the ability to write of the innermost closeness of heaven and Firmament and the descent of the Chariot, as the central master-concept of understanding the highest relationship of where God resides.

This mystical wisdom placed the Essenes as the aim of a holy life lived within the Covenant, was to penetrate the secrets of heaven in this world and to stand before God forever in the next age.

4th Dimensional Applications

The book of Enoch, not among the books included in the Torah Pentateuch or the Bible, serves as a reverence to the discovery of esoteric knowledge preserved by the Essene communities. Yet much of the esoteric knowledge has not been divulged for it was not secured among the Qumran caves.

The angel Uriel is utilized as a Time Traveler, able to travel to separate realities to link stories of past and present. This use of an angel was a unique writing skill set of the Essenes writers.

> **Uriel is utilized as a Time Traveler, able to travel to separate realities to link stories of past and present.**

The angel Uriel shows Enoch the cycles of the universe, making astronomy into the content of revelation. Astronomy is presented by a divine being, the angel Uriel. Cycles of the cosmos appear to have been edited into a story involving Enoch:

heaven wane and go down. And the fourth quarter, named the north, is divided into three parts: the first of them is for the dwelling of men: and the second contains seas of water, and the abysses and forests and rivers, and darkness and clouds; and the third part contains the garden of righteousness.

The book of the courses of the luminaries of the heaven, the relations of each, according to their classes, their dominion and their seasons. (Book Enoch, Chap 72-1)

What is not shared is the 4th Dimension thinking used by Essenes is to describe an event in a form that is perpetual, fluid, and non-static. The object moves as a lapse of time and immeasurable of the fluidity of its comprehension. The concept of Time is included in its cognizance, for Time becomes a measurable variable in this form of thinking. For the first event, Time in Travel is viewed in slices of non-linear fluid motion as it encompasses the ability to navigate in both past and future event capacities. This shared in the book *Shared Lives, Twin Sun* (2016).

A sample writing of 4th Dimensional thought is available in the description of the Portal of Light, an annotation of light and technology creation the shepherds followed to greet the newborn Messiah.

Use of the phrase, "Leafy Dawn Passage"-Angel is a metaphor for 4th dimension description of entryway or passage to view newly earthborn Messiah.

The description of the cave of the Messiah "Guarded by Angels" shares of the purpose of angels that guard humankind in specific instances. Angeles were a special favorite amongst the Essenes.

Use of unique writing skill demonstrates the writer's ability to connect the concept as the Portal of Light that links as sacred writings.

Infinite Knowledge - *knowledge Without Equal*

The Essenes considered themselves to possess *Knowledge Without Equal*. They spent much time in the study of both ancient writings and special branches of learning, such as education, healing and astronomy. An advanced intelligence, obtaining this wisdom from faraway traveler's welcome into their encampment. Knowledge from the East from India, Asia, Africa and undeveloped Western Europe were open to insight from all walks of life.

It is little wonder that the word Essene is not mentioned in the Torah nor the Bible.

Yet the esoteric foresight and nontraditional ways that knowledge is obtained and shared, causes the structured religions of that day to dismiss their advanced knowledge as nonsense. The efforts to suppress the knowledge of the ancestors of the Essenes forced the wisdom to be discretely shared among sheepherders, musicians, blue-collar workers, all aware that the enlightenment they conceal evolves from the disciples of the Creator itself, the Essenes.

At the beginning of the age of Aquarius, the Ladino-Sephardic community releases its knowledge of a Conscious Directive formula to create the Portal of Light in the Fourth Dimension.

The formula: Time + Direct Matter + Direct Energy = Conscious Directive

Time as a fluid basis of understanding of the Cosmic Time of the Fourth Dimension.

The *Semano*-heaven location is also revealed originating in the constellation Capricorn.

Abilities of Creator Illustrated in 21st Century

The twenty-first century will provide the ability of human's top astrophysics to grasp and explain how the Creator is able to manipulate Matter and Time to understand that a higher power does exist. This does not mean that the human astrophysics will be able to duplicate this higher dimensional skill set; this only reserved for the Creator level. The following are samples of skill sets utilized by the Creator.

How Portal of Light is Formed

The Creator is able to Manipulate both Light and Dark Light.

The manipulate of both Matter and AntiMatter is entitled Plank Technology, the ability of the use of Cosmic time in the Fourth Dimension.

This permits a Portal of Light to travel lengthy light-year distances and enter Earth's atmosphere described by the Angel Hermitaño as Shepherds follow the Portal of Light to locate the cave of the new Emmanuel.

Further Study

The real esoteric mysteries from the Essene scrolls reveal the ability to study further the writings of the books that contain mystical or esoteric knowledge. The mystery appears to include pragmatic issues of relationships between members, but more importantly, esoteric concepts known by the philosophical thinkers.

Phrases carried in Aramaic text, *the final Prince of the Congregation, or Royal Messiah*. Likely, refers to the miraculous birth of Noah. Without working knowledge of the Aramaic horoscope scroll, the subject could be many other biblical characters.

The book of Daniel is very similar in prose to the scroll of the Aramaic *Apocalypse Son of God* fragment (Vermes 4Q246), this fragment stating the *arrival of final ruler* would be imminent.

11

The New Messiah Ushers in Catastrophic Event Similar to Noah

The arrival of the New Messiah does not guarantee a cultural revolution of the political and social landscape to preserve the planet's historical values. Well into the age of Aquarius, there lies the possibility that a recognition that the Corporate Elite and AI have such control over the human values of society and the environment has been exploited to the point of no return, the new Messiah may assess that the Blue Earth is unable to be salvaged.

> *the new Messiah may assess that the Blue Earth is unable to be salvaged.*

Family values have ceased to have value in society as religious mores and institutions have been weaned to nothing. Developed country's native child's birth has drastically declined to mirror that of the leadership of the Corporate Elite. This means it cannot replace themselves and workers from foreign lands provide the growth of citizenship in most lands. This phenomenon will be a planned event by the Corporate Elite to create dependency upon AI. As the Creator-the Higher Being God appointed the new

Messiah to return the order to the planet, the decision of how the planet shall continue will prevail in the future with an assessment by the new Messiah. The determination of the depth of control of society by the Corporate Elite and support by the humankind as a whole will determine the course of action and directives to be provided by the new Messiah.

A clear sign that the Corporate Elite of developed countries have completed the exploitation of Earth and realize the planet cannot replenish itself, will be illustrated by the usage of Space programs of both public and private sectors continual practice of sending probes across the universe in an effort to locate a habitable planet. The ruling Corporate Elite will have recognized the eventual demise of the planet and spends a sizable amount of the budget to locate an exodus plan for their ruling elite.

The Believers must maintain their faith and spirit in the face of the Corporate Elite, to not relent even in secrecy; this is the key to preserving real faith. The new Messiah will search for these traits as a factor to salvage Earth. The Believers may look at the Sephardim Ladino's in New Spain as a model of preserving the real faith over hundreds of years.

The Essenes provides the description of persons of the Dark Light, from this vista, the new Messiah will be able to judge the degree that the Dark Light has engaged society and the ability to sustain a rebellion to rid the Corporate Elite.

The will of the people, the will of the fight to rid the Corporate Elite will play a part in this decision to fight the ruling Corporate Elite. If the obvious non-family values decisions of the Elite are not challenged, it is an indication that the Dark Light shadow has clear control over society.

If there is no will of faith, repressed by the control of media, education and social networks by both the Elite and the ever-adapting AI, the new Messiah may determine a more radical option may be the sole option to rid the non-Believers.

If there is no will of the Believers to combat the non-Believers and the Corporate Elite and support the organic environment, certainly the catastrophic event will be easily justified to the Creator Higher Being God of the necessity cleanse Mother Earth just as Noah expected in a previous time frame.

The Catastrophic Event

The Creator realizes that after a fire in the wilderness, nature brings back seedlings and growth at an unprecedented rate of new and fresh forest growth anew and provides for a new community that will initially respect the Word of God. This may be necessary to rid the Corporate Elite and AI. The original Believers and their offspring were not wise enough to stand up to the Elite and challenge them in a manner of fierceness and with conviction.

After the Great Flood of Noah, the people were scared and asked the Lord to never cleanse the Earth and *the Lord promised to never use waters to cleanse the Earth*. (Genesis 9:11)

To liberate the Believers, the most likely cleanse scenarios are fire and earthquakes remains the strongest possibility.

The environment has suffered and can no longer recycle the pollutants with healthy positive nutrients. The shadow of the Dark Light now has control over the wilderness. This again is an indication that no changes were made to challenge the Elites and the Oneness of spirituality has been largely ignored and outcast. The Creator will clearly place this blame at the fault of both Believers and non-Believers for permitting such disrespect of the Blue Planet that the Higher-Being Creator provided.

The Cleanse of Mother Earth

The new Messiah realizes that Earth itself has been exploited by the Corporate Elite and is beyond the reimplementation of values from the Creator, it becomes His or Her duty to cleanse the planet similar to Noah's Great Flood-the Deluge.

The Next Messiah brings forward a cataclysmic message of an environmental change to cleanse the land. The Lord has promised the scarred survivors of the flood-deluge would not happen again, yet a likely cleanse of fire and earthquake remains a strong possibility.

> *The Lord has promised the scarred survivors of the flood-deluge would not happen again, yet a likely cleanse of fire and earthquake remains a strong possibility.*

The likely scenario is a combination of fire from internal earth separating calamities or solar bursts causing fire and destruction, and the source does not matter. What is of significance is the petition of such a demise by the new Messiah. The scale of such an environmental firestorm will devise fear amongst developed countries that possess their nuclear weapons to be set off against one another, the former allies and this will contribute to the cleansing of the land.

It will be of most importance to identify before the arrival and influence of the new Messiah, those that are genuine Believers vs. non-Believers. For the works of the non-Believers is typically done openly with bravado and in the face of persons of faith. Also, pinpoint the identities of organizations or non-profits to provide leadership of the non-Believers, for they will cease identifying themselves as individuals. Especially egregious are those non-Believers that lead Faith organizations to further objectives of the non-Believing philosophies of the Corporate Elite.

Amazingly all lands will be set ablaze in the form of fire entitled Global Warming and cause ground separation via volcanic activity or earthquakes. Very few structures of a type will survive; the ruling Corporate Elite and AI will be held responsible for this calamity and will be among the first to perish. The Believers will be separated from the non-Believers, the Believers will maintain the last available resources to survive. The non-Believers will have to fend for themselves with few resources, many will now attempt to become Believers but will not be permitted.

Exit Plan for New Messiah

Is there an exit plan for the survival of the new Messiah to survive the cleanse as Noah Ark vessel that saved Noah's followers and a pair of each earth animal?

This would mean a vessel that can exist in the sea, or more specifically, under the sea in an Atlantis type of city or environment impervious to the above sea fire and burn of all existing land-based structures and animals? Are there to be two pair of each animal accompanied on this journey?

A covert and camouflaged Atlantis must be developed and hidden from the Corporate Elite in a location known to the Essenes as *a secret of man* carried in the Book of Noah (Vermes 4Q534).

The new Messiah will know the secrets of all of the living and know to place the new Atlantis in a location that aligns with the stars of the cosmos. This location will be locatable by a study of the light, the Sons' of light will be able to identity.

To avoid the upcoming catastrophic event is currently in the hands of humankind. Protecting both family values and the environment simultaneously, the axioms of Creation must be fought for and utilized to continuously challenge the non-Believers to prevent the Corporate Elite from taking control decisions that are detrimental to society. Comprehend that the importance of the Creation itself links to both prayer and nature, this Oneness of spirituality provided must be maintained at the highest levels at all times.

The Survival of The Believers

The new Messiah will provide an avenue of existence for the Believers. As with the Essene Book of Noah, the survivors were required to be descendants and were required to *abstain from shedding human blood and, on the ritual level, from eating animal 'flesh with the life, which is the blood, still in (Vermes Page 68 of 679; Community Law 1 the Covenant)*

Believers of today will be more diverse and not necessarily blood related but make no doubt, they will be genuine Believers. The Essene 's beliefs are based on Faith, NOT skin color. An avenue for existence will provide a journey with the new Messiah to protect themselves from the cleansing of mother earth. The vessel will ferry genuine Believers, not necessarily from the genuinely affluent or noteworthy, for safe passage to the remote location of survival.

> *genuine Believers. The Essene 's beliefs are based on Faith, NOT skin color.*

The vessel will be made of the original material foretold in the writing of the Portal of Light, a membrane of the matrix of a young star that was able to withstand the long journey from the heaven known as the *Semano*. The vessel can withstand both fire and water, provided by the Creator itself.

Upon arrival to the remote location, the new Messiah will require this small community of populace with the use of informational computer technology that will not possess priority over the fundamental values of the laws of Moses and the connecting Christian values entitled the Continuum. The Oneness of Spirituality with nature will be placed as the foremost priority. AI itself will be monitored to work with the limited scope of usage and require the Believer's consciousness will be influenced overall AI applications.

The grand mistakes of permitting non-Believers in complete control of social media, educational doctrine, Civil Rights and the corporate ethical decision, this perilous decision shall never be made again. The Corporate Elite maintained one common philosophy, a disconnect to Biblical values and placing persons to influential positions to provide a platform of social principles without religious values.

Believers' influence upon social media, educational doctrine and corporate ethical decision shall be applied to set boundaries not to permit the future non-Believer mores that exploited the social values of society. The strongly bound relationship revolves around the Continuum and beyond beginning in the Age of Aquarius.

Atlantis Ark

Living deep below the sea is the Atlantis Ark, the believers must live within this Ark that is self-sustaining similar to the nature of the original Garden of Eden. Until the smoke of the fire and ember has evaporated upon Mother Earth and the Cleanse is complete, the genuine Believers may reside in this adobe of their new home. Nature will seed itself in these embers of burnt Mother Earth and the genuine pristine Earth will return. At this point, the Ark Vessel may surface to view the landscape and locate favorable lands to restore humankind to a new environment with the painful lessons learned from disconnecting from both the Creator and nature.

12

I. What the Future Holds for the New Messiah

There will be a consolidation of religious groups in a society that is very much not religious society in the age of Aquarius. A politically conscious community of lawsuits and sensitive words takes precedence over historic values of family. Over time in this age, the non-Believers will have consistently whittled away at legal rights and family values that make America a society where the Easter and Christmas are considered historical holidays and the meaning of the existence has little value except to provide downtime in the hustle and bustle culture that exists.

> *A politically conscious community of lawsuits and sensitive words takes precedence over historic values of family.*

There will be many losses for the People of Faith that first seem small in stature such as the disingenuous civil right laws that permit the non-Believers to gain ground to justify their lifestyles or the training of school children from traditional Christian or Judaic homes into that the liberal non-Believers point of view is the new norm.

It is important to clearly understand that non-Believers decisions upon society are real losses to the people of real faith. Over time, these losses provide momentum to beliefs that hurt families and a certain point the non-Believers will possess the strength to make significant changes of institution norms that have been the backbone of American society.

The criterion of today's society is the understanding of this resolution, is the quest for equality of more prominence than the truism of liberty and freedom?

Non-Tax Status of Religious Groups will be Removed

In the very near future, the non-tax status of religious groups will be altered or removed and the typically low revenue producing secular orders will face real difficulty existing as organizations to serve people of faith. Due to this consequence, separate denominations will now be limited and there will exist two primary religious groups: The Jewish and the singularly Christians.

It is at this point the people of Faith will genuinely awaken and understand that the true objectives of the Corporate Elite and their ally AI, is to remove any significance of faith in society. It will be very clear; the Corporate Elites number one enemy is the People of Faith. Not a single shot has been fired and the survival of sectarian institutions is immediately threatened by the control of the non-Believers.

Sometimes a Great Loss is Needed to Learn a Lesson...

At the point of learning that the existence of their once untouchable church and temple structures are now at risk of closure, the Believers will have learned that it has taken a real tangible loss for the Believers to begin to galvanize and understand clearly this threat of the Corporate Elite.

The lesson learned is that the Believers clearly understand they must take back their rights to be individuals of conscious, yet it will not be easy. The non-Believers sway great influence over local and regional politics, religious values and virtues are treated as a concept of the past in society. Local and many State militia forces will enforce the laws established and expected to be enforced by the non-Believers. What is left to support the Believers?

> *The lesson learned is that the Believers clearly understand they must take back their rights to be individuals of conscious*

Families, yes, Families. Small cells of individual families that believe in prayer. This shall be the backbone of the resistance. The Lord listens intently on those whom follow the sacred word and pray for guidance in troubling times.

The now beaten down church and temple structures resemble the lonely adobe *Moradas* of the *Hermano Penitentes* of the American southwest, yet the faith continued. Families must step up and brace in arms in the candlelit churches and temples for the faith to continue. Standing aside will be the national military forces that do not commit to internal conflicts, yet for the prefect of all branches of their emblems is *God before all else*. These forces will not necessarily be controlled by the Corporate Elite.

A Familiar Friend in Salla in the Battle With the Corporate Elite

El Diablo-the Devil denounces, *I even lost the throne in furious battle to Daniel and Salla.*

There remains a possibility of outside assistance needed for the People of Faith. In the Exodus Play, mentioned there was a battle in which El Diablo-the Devil denounces, *I even lost the throne in furious battle to Daniel and Salla.* It is with this carefully veiled remnant of history, disguised as a bravado statement by El Diablo himself, that propelled the necessity to include the Islamic community in the battle to defeat the repressors of faith.

Daniel refers to the Judaic people of Israel from the Book of Daniel in the Old Testament. Salla refers to the Islamic prophet Muhammad Salla Allah Alai Wassallam and the Islamic community. In the battle of Uhad on March 19, 625 AD, Muhammad sought support from Jews (referred to as a group as Daniel) in the town of Midian (Northwesten Iran) in battle with vastly superior in number nonbelievers, those who opposed Muhammad. The nonbelievers do not believe in the word of the prophet Abraham. The battle contra the Elites and AI will be lengthy and challenging, the repression of the non-Believers will also bound the community of Salla.

For the participation and sacrifice of the community of Salla to defeat the non-Believers, Salla would have a chair at the table of decision making. Their voice shall be heard and heeded.

II. Future and Purpose of The New Messiah

The new Messiah has a primary purpose and reason for his or her arrival; support the healing of the separation and division of the Judaic and Christian communities.

How is this accomplished? For the new Messiah understands both sides and can clearly convince both the Judaic and Christian communities that they are of origin and one singular continuous faith and denomination, the Continuum.

Many apologies and forgiveness will emerge on both sides of this Continuum.

The Jewish community application of the concept of *mechilah*, forgiving of the other's indebtedness to facilitate this process. The Christian community application of forgiveness, this concept taught by Jesus of Nazareth. Not an easy process, yet it will get done for the existence of the new Messiah to flourish and the People of Faith to survive.

A lengthy and bloody battle between Believers and non-Believers will ensue to determine the leadership, control of planet Earth and the direction of Humankind.

The Elite and AI will possess the technology advantage that can, at times, be overwhelming within a battlefield, making Believers scurry in fear at the mere sight of metal soldiers.

The People of Faith will be more numerous in numbers and possess the advantage of faith as the backbone to stand up against AI, and this faith has provided for free democracies in both WWI and WWII battles on this planet Earth.

Yet the deciding factor that will provide the fate of the battle is the new Messiah.

The new Messiah will provide a combination of intellectual, social, esoteric and leadership blended skill set to assist in the battle against AI. It will not be your traditional war, rather fought in the gray or hidden across multiple battle lines in the effort to locate small pockets of AI's command posts. The most concealed post is AI's Central Command, where the networks are controlled to maneuver by non-Believers humans. Directing synthetic humans, metal solders, small battle machines, sophisticated listening and locating devices and drones, this post must always be located.

It will be quite an endeavor of form to locate this Central Command and the unique ability of the new Messiah, is to apply the concept of *Duende*-the art of performing at a high artistry level. This skill is locating this command center without being identified.

The Bridge

The historical differences between the Christians and Jews now have a common ground to share of the future with one another, the arrival of the New Messiah-Anointed One, providing a shared understanding just as the Essenes envisioned as in their battle with the Roman-Kitta.

An earthborn Messiah or Anointed One will be born to bridge or heal the discord between these historically rich theological communities to provide for the common goal of supporting the leadership and values of this new historical leader. The values of the genuine Believers will continue to flourish with the arrival of this Anointed One.

Final Victory

Upon leading the victorious People of Faith in the battle against Corporate Elite and AI, the new Messiah will only be available for a short time to be viewed by the community. The actions and philosophy fought for by the new Messiah will maintain the values and environment for the duration of the Age of Aquarius.

Imagine a healthy planet, values that reflect that of the Creator, families following the belief system of the Sons of Light. A planet that that embraces environmental protection of the clean waters, agriculture plenty for all peoples on Earth and deep respect of nature as many of the native indigenous cultures prioritize. The litmus test to determine if an environment is healthy, the organic and natural attraction of frogs. The innocent frog will not live in unhealthy environments with nature and noise pollution. Green space used to protect large tracts of land with limited capabilities for hunters and limited mineral rights options for forestry (replaceable forests) and oil and gas for specific and limited purposes.

Families that are unified by virtue of respect and their importance of the Creator will now look upon the computer processors with great pause. The anti-family values of AI technology will now be evaluated as to their importance and impact of the respect of families. Educational systems will now provide AI capabilities with family values as a top priority, this learned after permitting the Elites to change the historic values of society via AI efficiencies.

Private, public and non-profit boards of directors will always be evaluated to their real motives to influence all aspects of society. Unrestricted and autonomous selection of board members that mirror non-Believers shall NOT be permitted to direct their organizations that repress and exploit people of faith ever again.

The technology companies of both *applied* and *generalized* capabilities must be monitored as to their capabilities to control conscious and unconscious thought. The technology companies must be limited in their ability to work within areas that control free thinking of information and the ability to influence critical thinking. This limitation must also include foreign-owned companies.

Politicians MUST be trained and educated as to the ramifications of unmonitored AI capabilities and a new version of the Corporate Elite that arrives at the forefront to change society of the selected few.

What Is Important Today

What is important today is that the small battles matter to maintain the faith that must be existent and evident when the new Messiah does arrive, the new leader understands that genuine persons of faith have not given up or relented to the Corporate Elite.

It is the same commitment the *Ladino Hermanos* persevered to maintain the faith of the Law of Moses in the face of Christian repression. One thing that can be made certain, the Corporate Elite and their numerous boards of directors primary interest is in controlling the people of faith to be able to maintain and justify their life-styles. While this may be their strength, it is also their weakness.

People of faith must recognize the true objectives and motives of the Elite. At first glance, it may just seem like a group of leaders managing a non-profit or private organization. Look deeper at how their boards are situated and you will learn the ulterior motives go far beyond that of the organization and not of the long term benefit of people of real faith.

Yet ignoring the threats of the Elite at the beginning of the age of Aquarius will permit AI to be developed into the foe that persons of faith do not want to engage. The *applied* and *generalized* technology developed by AI at the beginning of the Age of Aquarius is not an intelligence to ignore.

The Appel Siri and Google Assistant will remove the individual conscious of faith to survive. The IBM Watson will learn to perform tasks that later become the solders and small warcraft of the future. All initially funded and supported by the people of faith; this technology was never questioned as to the future use of this intelligence.

The People of Faith must question the long term capabilities of both the Applied and Generalized capabilities of these now limited AI technology developments. Ask specifically, where does the individual conscious exist with the arrival of new capabilities of AI? Then, ask lawmakers to limit what capabilities are being developed in plain sight on the backs of the people of faith.

The individuals that support the Corporate Elite and AI of the future are the same individuals that exist today on various organizations and sit on the boards of directors. Learn to locate and identify their routines and practices, for this formula to change society to mirror their personal inclinations will not cease. One

> *Learn to locate and identify their routines and practices, for this formula to change society to mirror their personal inclinations will not cease.*

common identifying determinant, they are not real persons of faith or use faith as camouflage for ulterior motives. The second identifying factor, they prefer a top-down method of applying the Corporate Elite values, today they are small in number and work diligently to gain positions at the upper level of an organization to influence decision making on creating policy, administration of non-Believers philosophy and including voluntary positions to affect decision-makers view on their importance in a community. It is here you stand up for family values and their importance.

It is you as a person that does not have to go along with non-Believers discourse. Stand up and do not be bent by policies that are contra to your personal family values. Yes, expect to lose a contract or a position, yet this is the sacrifice that is required for real faith to be preserved.

It is important to understand where yourself or your family fit in this realm of life and its relationship to the development of AI by the Corporate Elite. If you use every technology provided by the Elites and do not ask, what are the long term consequences of this technology to myself and family? You can be certain a future model of Apple Siri will be able to control or limit your thinking by providing you with solutions that AI wants you to obtain, not the creative consciousness capabilities the Creator provided for objective and analytic thinking. Comprehend that buying the products or stocks of the institutions of the non-Believers will lead to the loss of individual consciousness and the rise of the Corporate Elite.

> *what are the long term consequences of this technology to myself and family?*

Spend time studying the affluent Corporate Elite that controls much of the decision making upon society and ask yourself, do the boards of directors of the Elites reflect the majority of Americans or myself? Yet want to lead and make decisions on the part of individuals in the community but are not elected but appointed by similar thinking Elites. The strength of private companies that affects the direction of society is enormous, the Facebooks, the Twitters, the Apples tell society how to communicate and provide the solutions to your questions, in effect control your destiny. Look objectively at the persons on the boards of directors and figure out the motives of their decision making. Challenge the board, for you will find they are appointed by top management and are typically non-Believers. Remember, you may buy stock in these publicly traded organizations and then question their leadership and decisions that affect society. Complacency provides the free reign of non-Believers to dictate society to meet their objectives.

In the end, it is families that will demand the ability to maintain their independence and think creatively and stand up to question the motives and real objectives of the non-Believers. Remember, non-Believers have weaknesses. One of their major faults is they lack a deep relationship with family members and many times must stand isolated. Pay attention, for their objective, it is ultimately is to remove your consciousness to support their lifestyles and objectives.

The Elite will take notice that you have not lost your independent consciousness of thinking and expect that you are identified and will single you out as a private enemy.

This shared via their comprehensive network of associates. AI will work very quickly and efficiently to mark you as a Believer and request their AI supporters outcast your actions, behavior and opportunities. Expect to be treated poorly, lack of job opportunities, exclusions from social groups, your writings or books banned by institutions, yet this is the price for freedom of the independent conscious and the ability to contribute to the concept of faith as part of society. For this demonstration of Faith is what the new Messiah will require to be part of the society of Believers upon his or her arrival.

III. Believers of Today

Respecting each other's church values is of utmost importance. What is necessary for Believers to coexist today is Believers keep arms-length away from other Believers churches. The primary reason is the lack of respect given to each other beliefs by written doctrine and the pouching of other Believers members. There is unnecessary time spent by pouching members of other Christian churches, for they have lost sight that the non-Believers are the real threat to their existence. The mega churches and Fee for Participation congregations have lost interest in real faith as demonstrated by Essenes. Should their leadership permit this knowledge of Spiritual Oneness to be shared with its members, the real solution of real faith as shared by the Essenes will reestablish their existence.

The Judaic Temple Believers also feel threatened by Christian pouching, the largest growing faithful in Israel today is Christianity. This is a real threat to the Judaic faith for the new Messiah will originate from this community, the new Messiah albeit he or she must be comfortable in a vibrant and healthy Judaic atmosphere to prosper.

> *the new Messiah albeit he or she must be comfortable in a vibrant and healthy Judaic atmosphere to prosper.*

The Judaic community must feel successfully autonomous in a world that threatens their existence. The Judaic faith has a unique history all its own; their faithful remember events of the past and incorporate these events into their life lessons of today. Respect and comprehend this form of faith and Christians must stop pouching and marketing to this community. The Sephardic Ladinos comprehends this lesson all too well and is one of the reasons for their survival to be able to relate a real-life story in anticipation of the new Messiah.

Christian Believers must challenge other Christian poachers and explain the purpose and values of non-Believers. Poachers existence is based on relationships they obtain from others; they must be boldly challenged by Believers and remove this ability from the relationship. Their friendly casual recruitment customs to invite you to events and begin a recruiting process must be challenged as a recruiting ploy and ceased.

The Believers Vs. The Non-Believers Going Forward

The next Messiah will possess a deep Judaic history that readily accepts the concept of the Continuum concept, the continuous relationship between the Christian and Jewish communities. Understand clearly that the preservation of the Judaic faith is essential in the 21st Century.

The real battle between Believers and non-Believers has left the starting gate and is now in full competition. Believers must now comprehend their focus is not upon other persons of faith, but those not of genuine faith that may hold themselves to be faithful, in actuality more political influenced followers.

Political parties and leaders that directly challenge family values must be questioned and challenged. It is not acceptable for political leaders to direct their followers to ignore deep-seated historical family values, they have placed themselves as non-Believers. A large portion of Essene community was non-married and continually believed and respected family values and their importance.

Political leaders must make their own real person decision, the continued leadership into non-family values on issues, and they must declare themselves political persons and not persons of faith. Politicos must be honest with themselves and discontinue labeling themselves as persons of faith, and rather their goal is enhancing non-family values by use of names such as diversity and opening society. They must honestly look at themselves and acknowledge their leadership identity is genuinely no longer of Christian or Judaic historical faith and leave that body of faith.

By the same criteria, Religious faith orders must challenge openly and directly those politicos that identify themselves from their order and are not genuine persons of faith. There is much confusion and lack of clarity from religious leadership that sit on their hands as politicos influence the conscious thinking of a congregation when they indeed are not genuine Believers.

With now advanced understanding of the Continuum of the Judaic Christian relationship and the potential arrival of the new

Messiah, those of the Congregation can politely ask the Politicos that attend service that they should consider leaving the faith of genuine Believers. The non-Believing Politicos have known for some time they do not follow faith doctrine for some time now and cling to their title of their faith in order to garnish votes. Being asked to leave their faith should be no surprise from either a Congregation member or Religious faith leaders.

IV. What Axioms Must Exist for the 21st Century

- Claim to the history of *La Merkavah* Chariot Descent.
- Recognize the direct relationship of Jesus of Nazareth and the Essenes.
- The arrival of the new Messiah will embrace the Continuum.
- Understand that the preservation of the Judaic faith is essential in the 21st Century.
- Prevent poaching of other Christian and Judaic faiths.
- The real non-Believers have little faith and or rely on political orientation for their identity; these are the groups that have priority to be recruited as a Believer.
- The Oneness relationship of Spirituality and Nature must be a priority.
- The Environment Must Be Healthy and Clean upon the arrival of the new Messiah.
- The *Nature Holders* being the Indigenous Native Communities around the globe, must be on board and believe that the Environment is made whole once more.
- Environmental programs and commitment must be made in the utmost expediency.

- The new Messiah known as the Anointed One will arrive and lead all genuine Believers.
- A healthy environment with genuine Believers will provide the basis for the new Messiah to begin preparing for the battle against the Corporate Elite and AI.
- The Corporate Elite's continued Exoplanet Exploration projects to locate another oxygen-rich Blue Planet demonstrates the lack of commitment to our Mother Earth. Be aware this research and commitment are at the expense of the biodiversity and health of our planet.
- Understand what is at stake if not prepared for the next Messiah. An unhealthy exploited environment and a society of non-Believers may provide for a singular decision by the next Messiah to abandon people of the Earth and watch fire erupt on this planet and end life as known.

13

The New Mother Mary Will Precipitate the Arrival of The Portal of Light

Mother Mary as Observer and Witness

The observation and witness of one mysterious person is never mentioned, Mother Mary. She would have been witness to a grand event, a Portal of Light appearing at the birth of her son, Jesus of Nazareth. The origination of the Portal of Light story may very well reside with this truly unique woman.

The Age of Aquarius' new Messiah will be earth-born; the timeframe and location of the birth will not be disclosed. The wisdom and expectation of a significant human and social event foretold by the Essenes will arise on behalf of the genuine People of Faith. Can a new Portal of Light be formulated to enter Earth's atmosphere and show shepherds the location of the new Messiah of the Age of Aquarius?

The answer is clearly, *Yes*. We are now able to view in amazement the capabilities of the Creator via Space Satellite photography that cannot be

> *Can a new Portal of Light be formulated to enter Earth's atmosphere and show shepherds the location of the new Messiah of the Age of Aquarius?*

understood or explained, sound familiar to the explained concept of *Duende*. This advanced technology should provide persons of the early twenty-first century the knowledge that a Portal of Light will enter Mother Earth's atmosphere, providing direction to a humble ensemble of shepherds as they traverse ravines and mountainsides to bear witness to the birth of the new Messiah. In modern days, these outside-the-box thought processes can now be confirmed by satellite telescope technology such as Hubble, Chandra-X Ray and Spitzer Space telescopes. Soon a lengthy light-year Portal of Light will be photographed by space satellites, and the understanding of this trapped light can be explained and even understood by the wisdom of early naked-eye astronomers.

The mystery will be how the Creator is able to develop such capabilities. For the Creator conceived our Earth and wants his/her creation of this Blue Planet to continue and prosper.

Can humankind duplicate this technology? The answer is No. As the desperate Corporate Elite seek to duplicate the powers of the Creator, they will come to realize they have violated the laws of the Creation and will face extinction themselves.

Unfortunately, many persons are not Believers and will not share in this marvel of the birth of the Anointed One, following politics of the Corporate Elite instead, challenging Creation with the advanced technology with the objective to control humankind and the Essene of the Blue Planet. These nonbelievers work upon projects of the Elite in hopes their efforts will preserve their nontraditional lifestyles.

Fortunately, the Creator loves humankind and will go to great lengths to protect his or her children. The Portal of Light shared in the Exodus Play and the Portals concept derived from the Book of Enoch may be far-fetched to some as a viable possibility, yet the capabilities of the Creator may never fully be understood.

Can a Nebula in The Constellation Capricorneus Create a Portal of Light?

The scientific Chandra satellite image below shares structures the astronomers referred to as "fingers," "loops," and "bays." These features indicated that the magnetic field of the nebula and filaments of cooler matter are controlling the motion of the electrons and positrons. The particles can move rapidly along the magnetic field and travel several light years before radiating away their energy.

Source: Chandra Satellite Observatory NASA/CXC/SAO; Optical: NASA/ STScI; Infrared: NASA-JPL-Caltech

The Nebula possesses the capability to travel lengthy light-years by use of a particle wind.

"When a pulsar moves through the interstellar medium, the nebula can develop a bow-shaped shock. Most of the wind particles are confined to a direction opposite to that of the pulsar's motion and form a tail of nebulosity. Recent X-ray and radio observations of fast-moving pulsars confirm the existence of the bright, extended tails as well as compact nebulosity near the pulsars. The length of an X-ray tail can significantly exceed the size of the compact nebula, extending several light-years or more behind the pulsar." -Source: Smithsonian Astrophysical Observatory https://www.cfa.harvard.edu/news/su201643

How Portal of Light are Capable to Arrive to Our Planet

The Creator itself will possess the capabilities to manipulate both Light and Dark Matter opposites to guide a propelled Light Vehicle. The Portal of Light has a special role in human existence, and it confirms the spiritual relationship of the Higher Being-God dimension entrance into our lower dimension existence of humankind.

The Portal is a conduit, a segue providing a message of enlightenment of such importance that it enters our atmosphere to illuminate the place of birth of a child whose philosophies, sacrifice and capabilities will forever change the human values of life on Earth.

2015 Drawing of the Portal of Light by Robert Maestas

The Light arrived from a higher dimension that created the Portal to be able to travel vast Light Year distances to shed light upon the birth of the Emmanuel.

The sound made by the Portal is reminiscent of sweeping leaves of a pathway with a millet broom yet following the rhythm of a three-quarter to six-eights count to the flamenco guitar standard of the Guajira travel genre.

The sound is appearing as the vibrating plank strands quivering as the portal enters our atmosphere, the plank interchanges with our oxygen-H2O rich atmosphere to create a unique chorus performed as one, almost as a backdrop of notes to the energy field itself.

Likely Reason Semano-Heaven Located in Capricorn Constellation

A likely reason that a burned-out white dwarf star was selected by the *Ladino Hermanos* as their *Semano*-Heaven was that a sister star is four times the size of our current sun in the same Milky Way galaxy. This sister star was located in the constellation Capricorn, a constellation with a known sister star, it is of significant importance for the story provides supporting evidence that the Portal of Light originates from this area.

Going a step further, the Creator used the large stars to manipulate a young star to create the Portal of Light that travels to the Earth's atmosphere and lead the shepherds to the cave of the birthplace of Jesus of Nazareth.

The Arrival of The Anointed One

To wonder at the arrival of the newly Anointed is truly a marvel of a truly unique and beautiful event in one's life. The genuine Believers will be awarded the warmth in their hearts and souls of the feeling that the new Anointed is forthcoming. It is a wonderful feeling reserved for those that did not relent and maintained their faith in this astonishing birth.

> *The genuine Believers will be awarded the warmth in their hearts and souls of the feeling that the new Anointed is forthcoming.*

Yet regardless of what news network garners your attention, those biased words will not protect you or your supporters from the reality that the new Messiah is sent with specific objectives established and required by the Creator. A new Mother Mary will give birth to a child; the Anointed One will arrive.

Conclusion

The Human Reevaluation of the Advent of Pandemics

The current life experience of this pandemic is a reevaluation of ourselves as Humans, and the Creator is sending the message, a *major blunder, you have disrespected our environment, exploited technology and may risk our developed life as we know it.* Society is now in fear that every time one steps outside of our safe place, you run the risk of bringing home a virus of death that informs you the Creator is not happy with our current state of affairs and is sending a message to his children of the Human race.

The advent of COVID-19, whether it be organically or humanly created, provides an exemplar of the stress that is being placed on our existence and environment. Can this be the start of a series of worldwide broad pandemic events that will challenge humankind before we seriously look within ourselves and genuinely reflect on both nature and our environment to see how we have blatantly disrespected ourselves?

> *you have disrespected our environment, exploited technology and may risk our developed life as we know it.*

Absolutely and Yes. What this means is that humankind must reevaluate itself and place boundaries on structural development, the technology of the environment and human decision making that reflects the organic requests of the Creator itself with few exceptions. The New Messiah will understand how to deal with this matter and the finger of responsibility will be pointed at those whom have created this pandemonium and the Corporate Elite on all sides of the political spectrum will be looked at hostilely

Spiritual Awakening Amongst the Reevaluation

The serious Pandemic that threatens our everyday liberties and freedom will recast the spirituality and a focused awakening that has not been witnessed since prior to WWII in these United States of America. An inner evaluation of ourselves and those around us will take hold. This will awaken our genuine spirituality and adjust those values that are important to ourselves and the focus upon our faith and religion will return. What will be recognized is what we have taken for granted, those that have maintained the genuine belief in the Oneness illustrated by the Essenes will be recognized for their diligence and sacrifice to preserve the connection of nature and spirituality.

> *This will awaken our genuine spirituality and adjust those values that are important to ourselves and the focus upon our faith and religion will return.*

The *Ladino Hermanos* provide the example of awaiting their faith by the expected arrival at the onset of the twenty-first century. The poor and humble adobe Moradas and rural homes preserved this genuine faith that one day the New Messiah will answer their pleas, awaiting one-half of millennia as did the *Ladino Hermanos*, this is what it takes to demonstrate the faith for this moment to arrive.

Persons of color, the Indigenous, Hispanic and African Americans will bear the brunt of this spread of fear and death due to disparities of health and feel most deeply the financial burden of the *Virus* for they do not possess the income or savings to withstand the long term affect upon society. The Millennial age group that currently does not connect to both religion and spirituality and resembles non-Believers will now be forced to adjust preeminent life decisions such as having kids or buying a home.

The Spiritual Reevaluation will hit square in the face those that feel most the financial burden of the Pandemic, the Persons of Color and the Millennials clarity will awaken and realize their situation in life is far beyond political and social doctrine. They will need to look within themselves and ask honestly if they are victims of society or do they plan to be real leaders and search for the New Messiah and the historic deep-seated Judaic-Christian values that will lead them out of harms way.

Time has a Way of Providing Remedy

The real crux for this book, is the application of the concept known as the Continuum. This term was used by the Jewish scholars that in vain attempted to convince Queen of Isabella of Spain of the continued or continuum relationship between the recognized Christ, Jesus of Nazareth and the historic Jewish history.

> *The real crux for this book, is the application of the concept known as the Continuum.*

The Queen would have nothing to do with this relationship, thus born were the *Sefardim*, the Jewish community that was the target of expulsion to all parts of the world. What the Queen and her supporters did not realize is that the community she was expelling included those that maintained the Jewish mystical properties and the study of the Kabbalah that derived from the Essenes.

With this writing of this work, as any Rabbi will explain to you, is the shared ability to request freedom from repression by the petition by virtue of the Anointed One known to others as the next Messiah. This is exactly what transpired, for the wisdom and memories of the Jewish can span ages of time regardless of the repression or time frame we live upon.

As we enter the 21st century or age of Aquarius, the Anointed One will be of Judaic faith, requested by the repressed Ladino community. Time has a way of providing a remedy. As a giving and understanding Anointed One, this leader will recognize the concept of the Continuum.

Expect the Birth of The Anointed One Tomorrow

The Bedouin boy that discovered the chards of vase pottery ultimately discovered the origin and roots of the Judaic-Christian origin, yet also the foretelling of the arrival of the new Messiah at the beginning of the age of Aquarius.

The Essene community that slew themselves at the arrival of the Roman-Kitta not only concealed their past by burying their many scrolls near their Masada fortress, but this act also continued to disguise the family roots of one Jesus of Nazareth and the ability for historians to reveal the expected arrival of a New Messiah that will be known as the *Anointed One* at the beginning of the 21st Century.

The clue foretelling of the Anointed One was provided in a repressed and concealed Christian play entitled the *Exodus Play*, providing a light that has not subsided since I read he unforeseen yet carefully placed revelation in the play, *How is she to be treated*?

What this women will witness is the Portal of Light and its' Millet sound, the Shepherds as Angels, the Animals as Humans, the *Leafy Dawn Passage* as the Light of the Lord guarded by the angels Michael and Rafael and all observed by the time traveler angel Uriel.

The key to grasping this foretelling is once again the next Mother Mary, for prior to the birth of an expecting child, the expecting Mother Mary must be an observer of the events that will proceed with the birth of the special child.

Yet to be born in the advanced technological age of Aquarius, the new Herod will now be the entity of the Corporate Elite and Artificial Intelligence. The question, "How is she to be treated" has been answered, the non-family values and faceless corporate values will pursue this child to be born and once again, Mother Mary will be on the run hoping to locate a rural setting along the 33° latitude.

The newly born Anointed One will answer the calls of the Judaic community, born of a Judaic being and faith. I first ask the Judaic followers not to be initially alarmed that this is not an *end of times* or apocalypse scenario. Truly enjoy this special birth, for the smiles upon the Judaic faces and homes will last an eternity. Yes, there will be countless dancing in the streets for the inner joy on behalf of the Judaic child is in fact, the Anointed One that has been awaited for well beyond ages.

This birth does not arrive without its challenges and reasons. The 21st and 22nd century will challenge the existence of organic humankind itself. The new Anointed One will arrive for precisely this reason, to lead humankind to survive this onslaught and, once again, demonstrate the values for humankind to follow for their existence.

Yet there is a great risk for humankind, nature and the environment are all a child of our Creator. The disrespect and stress placed upon our *Blue Planet* provide for a scenario that the Anointed One may realize that our species has forgotten, the Oneness relationship of nature and spirituality. There remains the possibility that Noah's Great Deluge of now fire and smoke may be the course set by the new leader to cleanse society and rid the influence and power of both the Corporate Elite and Artificial Intelligence.

To Know The *True Israel*

To genuinely understand the *community* known as the Essenes, once must peel back the exterior of an existential callous and raw living and view a fraternity of men whose primary goal was to enclose themselves to both nature and especially water in a parched desert environment. Devoid of attention by most observers, what was not shared, what did this community know that was forthcoming, what sacrifices would be made to conceal *True Israel*.

This community connected spiritually and intellectually to nature like no other, their ability to create, preserve, study and work with the sacred writings of Moses will never be surpassed.

It is little wonder they were asked to preserve the scrolls near their fortress of Masada.

What not shared is their awareness that at the beginning of the new age, the age of Pisces, they were aware that one of their kindred would produce a living being that would possess the advanced healing capabilities of the brotherhood and the depth of knowledge of this community. This earth-born child would be like no other, yet, it was never to be shared or acknowledged.

The family tradition was truly Essenian, one that produced the rebel, the stubborn and undeterred opine known as John the Baptist. He to knew that the coming of this new age would provide a human being that possessed capabilities never before witnessed prior or after this birth.

The Nazarene was known for his pureness of heart; in a time where the bodily illness was the norm, he healed all whom approached him. The Nazarene understanding of philosophy derived from the community that educated him, the Essenes. He was aware that the majority of society would shun his abilities, for they would realize he derived from Galilee, this northern region of Judea, that maintained the raw strength of the Essene community. Yet quiet was this family that created the Baptist and the Nazarene, for this immediate family of women, men and children knew their lives were also in danger. Followers at a distance and at the darkness of night, they knew a grand sacrifice was to be made by both men. The Essene community within the Masada followed the same sacrifice at the arrival of the Roman-Kitta.

No mention was made of a relationship between the Baptist or the Nazarene to the Essenians or from the scrolls themselves; the understanding of sharing of this relationship would endanger the entire family. The word Essene has never been mentioned in either the Torah or the Bible.

> *The word Essene has never been mentioned in either the Torah or the Bible.*

Yet there it was, in full view for those that peel back existential living to see *True Israel* and the community of where it originated. The unidentified and anonymous *Teachers of the Masada*, paved the road for those that are able to *See*, the beginning of the next leader of pureness of heart. To foretell the future is an observational skill, the Essenes share this capability for those who wish to be *Shown how to See*, as Vincent Van Gogh described.

What the Future Holds, The Grand Purpose

The arrival of the new Messiah, the Anointed one, will arrive for a grand purpose.

Think of the Anointed One's arrival with the environmentally crafted skills to care for nature with loving and compassionate beliefs, to heal and protect our mother, *Blue Earth*.

The harsh reality going forward into the 21st century, the Corporate Elite will desire a society that is reflective of the values of themselves, less family-oriented, fewer children, work-driven, and the dependency upon AI to make life easier to manage.

This quintessential story will be broadcast at the dramatic cost of our environment.

Is the New Messiah expected to be the Anointed One for War or Peace?

This is the million-dollar question?

Few persons seek the Anointed One to be a leader of war or of the final Armageddon.

The grand purpose is the reality that the Creator will place a premium on our environment and the primary factor for the existence of newly Anointed One is to protect our *Blue Planet*.

Jews Will be Expected to Fight Physically

The newly Anointed One will be of Judaic background and this places special responsibilities upon this community.

In the battle to oust the Moors from the Iberian-peninsula in the middle ages, most of the Jewish community were the administrators of the Monarchy and not the battle soldiers. Queen Isabella and her supporters recognized this event and took measures to rid the thought of as non-Believers as part of the final reconquest of Iberia. This event will not repeat itself and the Judaic community will be expected to fight physically against the Elite and AI. This will ensure the Judaic participation among leaders upon the final victory alongside the newly Anointed One.

> *This will ensure the Judaic participation among leaders upon the final victory alongside the newly Anointed One.*

The Arrival of The Pandemics

The sudden arrival of a virus pandemic that can cripple the economies of first world's developed countries in a matter of weeks, this illustrating how our planet is vulnerable to a human species extermination.

The disruption of supply chains of foods and meats, inability to cleanse home and work environments and the sudden spread of illnesses that can place safe homes at risk, will create chaos our world has never witnessed.

This dilemma will give new meaning to an old word; the *take out* of meals, foods and all other retail services will be handled handless. It is quite unfair to place the risk of the virus being spread upon food workers, health service persons and financial service persons. New will be the required use of an adjusted and reworked concept of *taking out*; everything you need will be submitted online to obtain foods, banking transactions, retail transaction and then picked up by yourself or another from your home to decrease the risk of the spread of the *virus*.

This concept of handless transactions will soon encompass all neighborhoods throughout the globe. A series of Pandemics will alter the very fabric of life as we know it, the continual visit to the corner kiosk to have a long cotton needle entered into your throat and tested to see if you have one of the many mutant viruses's within your body will determine if you must alter your daily ritual and obtain the new vaccine or go into quarantine for two weeks.

The Pandemics will provide one major change in human values, and we will no longer take for granted gifts provided by the Creator, this ungrateful act must absolutely stop. The supply chain interruptions and hoarding of life-essential products will provide the understanding of the importance and appreciating of everyday products that make our lives enjoyable.

> *we will no longer take for granted gifts provided by the Creator, this ungrateful act must absolutely stop.*

The bounty of healthy crops, freshwater, clean air will be respected, helping other communities or countries in the sharing of these gifts will make our entire world society better. This specifically does not mean we shall use government or communal forced concepts to complete this task, rather the real beauty is the intelligence and freedom to create a healthy environment that will be used to share these gifts.

The idolization of sports, arts and entertainment figures will have a new assessment; it will no longer be based upon social and media attention in connection to the salaries commanded by these artist figures. The new appraisal will be based upon the genuine individual art skill possessed by the artist and their contribution provided by the artist to improve the lifestyle of humanity and our environment. The genuine contributions to humankind by the legitimate gifted artists is a sharing their genius, these offerings will ensure that the intrinsic values will be a part of society for our *Blue Planet* to survive and prosper as the Higher God intended.

This new matter world is of most importance, the modified artistic attitude to improve humanity and our environment prior to the arrival of the New Messiah, will provide an understanding that Earth's society has adapted a philosophy of preservation and sustainability of our Blue Planet.

New Constitutional Amendment

The advent of the Ultimate Battle will necessitate that the Constitution of these United States be amended to ensure that the non-Believers inaccurate faith, philosophy and use of AI, never be permitted to gain control of society in any capacity in the future.

Our Forefathers in our Constitution, specifically wrote two amendments to protect religion, the *Establishment Clause* and the *Free Exercise Clause*, the new amendment will place religious freedom and conscious in control of genuine Believers.

A second new amendment will prevent the non-family values attributions of the Corporate Elite to be limited to prevent the return of their values and exploitation of genuine family values to be repressed once again.

The Second Coming of Christ

The Christian concept of the Second Coming of Christ revolves in broad terms around biblical references by Luke and Acts (Luke

24-36b, Acts 3:12-19), *Christ has Died, Christ has Risen, Christ will Come Again.*

As the Jewish faith has anticipated patiently for the Anointed One to arrive, this is their time, the Age of Aquarius, the arrival of the secret truths of the Essenes has now disclosed the foretelling of this upcoming event.

The Time of the Constellation Ages is lengthy upwards +2,000 years, and this does not mean that the Second Coming of Christ will not occur, just not at the beginning of the 21st century known as the Age of Aquarius.

More importantly, the influence and impact of the work of Jesus of Nazareth will continue into the 21st century and beyond, this will be recognized and valued by the Anointed One and be known as the Continuum.

Solutions for Today

At what point will humankind realize that the overdevelopment, overpopulation density, and dependency upon fossil fuels will lead to a series of pandemic viruses that our economies cannot endure. Interestingly, the arrival of the new Anointed One coincides with this pandemic environmental crisis.

The solution always began and resided with the indigenous communities that live amongst economically depressed homelands and reservations. These communities have never forgotten the Oneness of nature and spirituality. Yet for this conviction and cherished understanding, they are looked down upon as not intelligent, not part of the advanced society and rarely valued as a community, yet dutifully this community has protected the solution to preserve the existence of humankind.

Adopting the *Way of Life* of an indigenous community that must be brought forward to the American lifestyles is the realization of the respect of traditional organic families and the environmental relationship of nature and spirituality, which will provide a prosperous and healthy ambiance the New Messiah would acknowledge and appreciate.

> *recycle centers will be a significant priority and the Kosher handling and cleanliness*

The long-held story of the American Buffalo upon capture would relinquish all components of their body to be freshly consumed or recycled for another day by the indigenous community, this concept a priority for today's society. In our modern society, recycle centers will be a significant priority and the Kosher handling and cleanliness of all items used once will be recycled many times over. The family event to attend and praise of items provided by humankind will be reminiscent of the customs of the indigenous communities.

Prayer and Nature

Prayers for the elements provided to maintain our communities, adapted from the customs of the Essenes, prayer before and after meals will become a custom. The connection to the elements of what we eat and prepare to our Creator and Give Thanks is

> *prayer before and after meals will become a custom*

one of the keys that must be emphasized and will be appreciated by the New Messiah.

Our societies currently lack the bond with nature and spirituality, and genuine prayer will summons and prioritize this relationship. This comprehension of prayer and nature is what made the Essenes special. In our modern societies, it not been made a priority and yet a preeminence within Indigenous communities. This must be made clearly understood and practiced for a healthy society to flourish.

The Anointed One will observe and appreciate the sacrifice made by these indigenous communities to maintain the bond of nature, the environment and spirituality. For some may only recognize the bond as a custom to the new Messiah, this is a genuine sign that the original purpose of the Creator has not been forsaken.

The Arrival

The arrival of the Anointed One will be early in the twenty-first century, as mentioned, the location and community born will not be disclosed. For those expecting a series of events as

> *The Anointed One will provide trust in the shared belief of the writing in the esteemed sacred writes of both the Bible and Torah.*

identifiers prior to arrival or birth of the special one, this writer requests that you look closely at the Time Frame that coincides with the earnest request of this new Messiah to arrive at the bequest of the genuinely silenced and *repressed Ladino Hermanos*. For this brotherhood maintains the qualities of life that kept secret this forthcoming birth event, this parallel to the Essene community of life that kept secret the birth event that took place in their forthcoming birth of the Nazarene in Judea.

The Anointed One will provide trust in the shared belief of the writing in the esteemed sacred writes of both the Bible and Torah. This trust is essential for, in times of both challenging economic and faith hardships that we find ourselves, you will know and can maintain conviction in the exact virtue of the Believers will prevail and again stand the test of time.

The Author's Note and Background

When the Exodus play first arrived to me back in 2011, I asked myself simply was why me?

For whatever reason, this story permits me to touch into my Judaic history and share what is felt and told from ages past. I can't explain it, for it does take what we call in my community *"cojones"* or fortitude to delve into a community of repression and hurt and share this story.

Why would a story sharing disclosing of the arrival of the new Messiah or the Anointed One be placed in my hands to be shared with the community? Those readers able to recognize the lengthy history of repression of the Jewish community, this story may have preserved and provided for the foretelling of what will happen tomorrow.

At a relatively young age from a rural community, I sought out the wisdom, preserved the knowledge and grasped the Essene of the Sephardic Ladino community known as the *Seranitas*. This endeavor provided the understanding that cryptic wisdom derived from the Judaic history of the Cosmos and the application to humankind.

As a state of Colorado native, I do want to disclose time I spent working and dealing with all major Department of Defense companies in the United States of America. Specifically, I was able to contribute to the assemblage of a Space Satellite that currently flies in our cosmos; this a very special insight to our understanding of the configuration of our cosmos. The awareness of working on various programs and dealing with security clearances has provided insight that most Americans rarely obtain access. This may contribute to myself being selected to share of the insight and *Enlightenment* of the Anointed One.

With this historic knowledge and understanding of the arrival of the next Messiah or the Anointed One, the events of laws of today and society tell me the next leader will be a leader of battle contra the Corporate Elite and Artificial Intelligence.

The Exodus play came to me long before the writing of this fifth book when I was simply asked to share and reveal the concealed community that is expecting the arrival of this Anointed One and the application of the concept known as the Continuum. A phrase in the Exodus plan that concealed the advent of this arrival forever changed my understanding of how our world actually flowed. It was this camouflaged story that provided the impetus to reveal the writings on this Essene theological evolution connection of both past and future. Sharing that life-altering revelation became imperative in writing this book.

Telling of a future manifestation, regardless of its purpose, often is not a welcome event. Grand life events possess their own timing and reason for their timely appearance, irrespective of your current social and political status, as we see with the effect of this

Pandemic – it does not discriminate. These life events are entirely out of one's control, as is the advent of a specific historical figure in the Age of Aquarius and the coming of the Anointed One.

This book is timely to give answers to those touched by the Pandemic and this gradual loss of control of one's privacy and individuality and ability to keep control of our lives because of the encroaching suffocating technological AI embraces in the guise of helping mankind. The digital age of AI is this century's Trojan Horse—and it will kill you. This book attempts to make sense of why this is happening, what to expect and what each person can do to combat it by understanding the forces put into play millennia ago by higher power and intelligence.

The book also contains history, riddles, stories and tales, heroic people, warnings, faith, and a new way of considering our skies and earth that the ancients already knew – we have but to LISTEN. Anthony Garcia is a majorly serious historian, writer, visionary, teacher, musician and creative artist. With deep southwestern New Mexico and Colorado roots going back to the beginnings of the Ladino culture established there, he resides in Denver but often travels to the land of his heart and "*alabados*".

Specific to mention is my experience with what is entitled, the *Cancel Culture,* a broad term coined for a broad cultural community that works jointly to suppress creative works that do not agree on a particular point of view or philosophy. Most of my works have felt this broad stroke of *Cancel* philosophy, for my works are either repressed or not permitted to be illustrated. Denver Public Library has boldly displayed this skill to my pen, others just work as collective council of sorts, this skill foretold as a Corporate Elite form of control and disregard of our 1st Amendment. Do not fret those of the membership of *Cancel Culture*, the New Messiah, the Anointed One will make special note of this effort.

His four published books have garnered much attention, acclaim and awards.

The Portal of Light, (www.ThePortalLight.com) has won numerous awards, including USA Book Gold awards in the classification of History and Religion categories and is a finalist for the New Mexico Book Association for the Religion category. The book is historical non-fiction of the cryptic journey of the Judaic community of New Mexico and Southern Colorado. The Colorado History Museum carries *The Portal of Light* as part of their permanent collection library. The website for this book receives over 2,000 new hits from curious buyers each month.

Released in the fall of 2016, *Sacred Lives, Twin Sun*, a companion book to the *Portal of Light*, brought the story to our current time of the spiritual mystery of the Ladino influenced directive into the modern world and garnered winning awards including USA Book Silver awards within the Religion categories.

The novel *Watili, the Native American Slave Heroine*, (www.Watili.com), was completed in the late fall of 2017 and is carried by both Barnes and Noble and the Tattered Cover book stores.

The *Word Decoder* (www.WordDecoder.com) was completed in spring 2019, a historic fiction Young Adult prose that has drawn the interest of readers passionate about the environment and indigenous native connections. The book received the coveted 2019 *Best Cover* from the Colorado Independent Publishers Association. *Artificial Intelligence and The New Messiah*

Garcia is also an astute observer of our society, his passion for concerns of our survival and future of humanity has spurred him to this fifth book, ARTIFICIAL INTELLIGENCE AND THE NEW MESSIAH: It Was Foretold – Are We LISTENING? It is of the connection of the history of cryptic Jews from the *Portal of Light* insight to the Dead Sea Scroll discoveries in Judea written by the Essene community inscribed prior to the first century BC. (www.ArtificialIntelligenceandNewMessiah.com)

Anthony Garcia is founder of Twenty First Century Investments and Benefits, located in Denver, Colorado and holds an M.S. in Finance, an M.S. Minor in Health Administration and his B.S. in Business, all from University of Colorado. A veteran of theatrical and musical performances and numerous book signings and lectures, he is an ideal candidate for interviews and travel to promote his book.

Afterword

I do not write in professor speak, or intellectual depth for only a certain higher level educated person can solely understand. My prose is specific in design for the man or women that seeks to understand the big picture and to grasp. the arrival of a forthcoming historic event and a window of time that will allow both individuals and families the election of being either a Believer or non-Believer.

This writing shares the purpose of two specific events:
1. New Messiah will soon be born in the early twenty-first century;

2. The Essenes steadfastly concealed both the family and the arrival of the Messiah at the beginning of the first century and provided for the model to not disclose the window of the arrival of the next New Anointed One to soon be born.

This book be used as the bridge between the Christian and Jewish communities to bond in anticipation of the significant historical and social forthcoming event.

The recent event of the Covid-19 Pandemic provides an anticipatory notice or calling card for the human race, expect significant challenges to your own viability in the near future.

Our *Blue Planet* has met its capacity to clean and renew itself as if a carburetor filter, the sponge has met its limit and a virus will take hold of human bodies, the expectation of future clean, renewable air and water may not be possible in the future.

Many a reader may not comprehend the message of this book, many readers will not want to share this book, many readers just do not want to accept they are not a Believer, and maybe it is best for my own personal safety to not share this foretelling of events.

But as always, I have done my job and share the forthcoming events and how the history of the Essenes had led to the influence and writings of the Judaic faith and the disclosure of the New Messiah by the *Ladino Hermanos*.

There is hope, that will only come with a significant change of how our planet is treated. I can tell you with certainty that the new Anointed One will also do his or her job. A planet that is unable to cleanse itself and the continual virus breakouts that are labeled plagues, yet in actuality, are cloaked stepped time limit markers of the telling of our future existence.

If you genuinely want to provide the viability of yourself and family, flood the capital of each town and city with the community and do what has worked in the past, a *Sit-Down* and DO NOT LEAVE for weeks until the significant changes and resources provided to make this planet entirely healthy.

Anthony Garcia

Addendum A

The Future Shared in the Technology of the Portal of Light

The purpose of Addendum A is to demonstrate for further study how both Kabbalists and members of the Essenes would use Arithmetic or Counting to calculate to identify or conceal within the cosmos their knowledge of Astrology in Section I.

The use of Angels are commonly employed as Guardians or Messengers, they were further adopted to explain and identify Portals or Openings within the Cosmos or Heaven itself. For the future important concepts or the arrival of historical persons will be located by use of the Apertures, Openings or Portals. This explained in Section II.

I. The Counting of Astrology:

What is cryptically hidden in the Book of Astrology is the number counts and sequence of places or items of the story of heavens that Enoch is sharing with those that understand the secret coding. The Count will provide an arithmetic count of the science of the cosmos.

This means nothing to the casual reader, yet means a significant clue as to the sequencing, the steps or, count that will provide a corner point or count to a specific sequence to a location within a constellation. The cryptic story begins with an unknown variable. Clues are provided to count arithmetically from a clue point along a constellation line of stars or count points to arrive at a destination.

Specific astrologers of Arabic descent count by use palmas-hand claps in a musical rhythm to count the sequence from a corner point to locate a specific destination along a celestial drawing line.

Flavius Josephus supported this method of sequencing as he commented,

He communicated to them arithmetic, and delivered to them the science of astronomy; or before Abram came into Egypt they were unacquainted with those parts of learning; for that science came from the Chaldeans into Egypt, and from thence to the Greeks also ... (Antiquities Chapter 8-2)

The Arithmetic Clues to the Cosmos
Clues to the Sephardic Heaven

What is missing, not located nor disclosed among the Dead Sea Scroll findings, is a ledger or contents page that reveals the clues that would provide a beginning point to locate the constellation or celestial location to begin the Count. Without the ledger, intimate clues would be left within the writings to establish a starting point to discover sacred knowledge of the Essenes' scrolls.

The example of the Exodus play, the cryptic clue was the phrase,

Barvaro de Semano--The Old Beard in Heaven

Initially, this meant nothing. Only an out of place phrase that had little or no meaning. Actuality, proving to be the primary clue to point to the location of the constellation, and it the Sephardic heaven.

The clues provided questions to provide a solution to this riddle:

1. What constellations possessed Beard?

Answer: The half man-half horse constellation Capricorn possessed the beard of the man and whiskers of the horse.

2. Where was the starting point?

In the Exodus play, two clues that provided the starting point:

a. *Un seis entre estos pastores*—one-six of between these shepherds

b. 33° Parallel

The star Dabih Major located in the Capricorn star group, followed by the latitude parallel line of 33° North and 1/6 from the corner point of the star assembly. It is the exact same place as the whiskers of the Sea Goat of the Constellation.

The Semano–heaven was located in the area of the Sun Capricornus on the constellation Capricorn.

II. The Portal and Angel Uriel

The Portals in the Book of Astrology are best described as Openings into the heavens or the Chariot. For example

The Heaven: *the luminary the Sun has its rising in the eastern portals of the heaven,* (Book of Watchers, Chapter 72-1).

The Chariot: *In like manner twelve doors Uriel showed me, open in the circumference of the suns chariot in the heaven,* (Book of Watchers, Chapter 75-4)

How the angel Uriel was used in the Book of Astronomy

1. *As a Guardian to protect Garden of Eden*
So he drove out the man; and he placed at the east of the garden of Eden Cherubims, and a flaming sword which turned every way, to keep the way of the tree of life. (Genesis 3-24)

2. *As a Messenger*
God charged Uriel with announcing to Noah the "end of flesh" (Book of Watchers, Chapter 10-2)

How the Angel was used in Exodus Play

In the Exodus play, an angel, likely Uriel is used for similar capacities:

1. As Guardian to protect the Portal entrance to the child Messiah
The portal is deep and has a guardian. The child is young, he is the promised Messiah. (Page 190, The Portal of Light)

2. As a messenger to the Hermitaño
An angel has told us. The Messiah was born in Bethlehem
(Page 158, The Portal of Light)

3. The suddenly appearing Hermitaño character himself is likely an angel providing leadership and wisdom to follow the entrance of the portal of light.

In the Exodus play, the Ladino/an authors employed Hermitaño angel as a Guardian, Messenger, and Leader following the Portal of Light, this concept learned from the early writings in the Book of Astrology.

This validates the authors of the Exodus play had access to the Book of Astrology, their ability to write in esoteric form, and conceal variables to share among the Sephardic community. The authors were able to conceal wisdom in three formats:

1. In written form, shared among Sephardic community

2. Oral tradition between Sephardim *Hermanos de Luz*-Brothers of Light.

3. The singing of the beautiful and veiled message laden Alabados.

How Angel was used to follow the Technology of the Portal of Light

In Kabbalah inspired book, *Shared Lives, Twin Sun*, the Count was used to locate the Sephardic Heaven known as Semano from clues left openly concealed in the Exodus play. Later, the open clues were used to reconstruct the technology of the Portal of Light and to explain the arithmetic equation of a Conscious Directive:

Time + Direct Matter + Dark Energy = Conscious Directive

This advanced theory, uses the story of the ancient Portal of Light, explained in the usage of Plank Technology, to share futuristic events are that will come to light in the 21st Century.

Appendix A

How the Exodus Play Relate to Characters relate to the Essene History

Tubal (great grandson of Noah) was the direct descendent of a prominent Judaic person and link to the Great Flood referred prominently by the Essenes in Genesis Isiah, Deuteronomy, Zechariah, Acts and Proverbs.

Hermitaño the time traveler from the Exodus play, provided the direct link to the Book of Astrology and the time traveling angel Uriel that is used in the same manner as the Hermitaño in the Portal of Light.

A Hermitaño character statement, a *Dream that landed him in this time frame* within the play, a parody patterned after Enoch's use of the angel Uriel visit to view the cosmos and the Universe.

The Hermitaño led the shepherds as they followed the Portal of Light to greet the Emmanuel with gifts and effigy. This Light originating from the secret Ladino word known as the *Semano*-the Heaven, brought wisdom and a mature, authentic history of infinite knowledge to his persona that the shepherds entrusted and followed under the guise of the Portal of Light

Hermitaños as a group linked as angel traveler in books of Daniel, Matthew, Psalms and Corinthians.

Lepio, a character linking to sacking of First Temple by the Romans, in books of Job and Daniel.

Angel (Michael and Rafael) made reference to the strong relationship between Michael and the Messiah. Used as links to Isiah and Ecclesiastes.

Angel El Diablo-the Devil (Belial aka by the Essenes) drove the story and his phrases touch upon every major and minor reference in both the bible and Torah. Yet, the real importance of the devil telling a Christian story is the Christian masquerade of tolerance and love of others and the pursuit of the Jewish people as heretic makes the Devil the appropriate person to tell this Christian story.

The Essene community was also repressed and outcast by the dominant Pharisee group in Judea.

Jila states in Portal of Light play, referencing the next Messiah: "The sacred Maria, the beautiful child, they say the most beautiful without equal, so that if another is offered as she, how is she to be treated?"

The Essenes also awaited an earth born Messiah to arrive at the beginning of the age of Pisces, this analogous to the awaiting of the new Messiah in the new twenty first century of the age of Aquarius.

Carnation-camouflaged name for Jesus of Nazareth
Will the new Messiah in the age of Aquarius be referred to as the Carnation?

Daniel Refers to Torah writer Daniel and the Judaic community as a whole.

Salla The word refers to Salla Allah Alai Wassallam, the Islamic Prophet Muhammad and the joint battle alongside Daniel, a Judaic person against the non-believers in 625 AD.

Biblical Locations as Part of Exodus Play

Rúbal: The word Rúbal is placed without reference to anything specific in the play and initially disclosed the word applied to Rúbal al Khalid, the great sand desert in present day Saudi Arabia and providing a clue as to the a location for the story of the play that would become the lightly snowed Sinai mountains and the journey to Bethlehem had its origin.

Uhad: *I even lost the battle to Salla and Daniel*—El Diablo
   The battle took place in Uhad in northwest area of Rúbal al Khalid desert.
   The Battle of Uhad today is still visited by the Muslim community as a historic event celebrated as a victory over non-believers.

Snowy Mountains: Reference to Mount Sinai mountains other side or Rúbal al Khalid desert.

Tree of Life: Reference from Kabbalists Moshe Cordoviero or Isaac Luria, Adam and Original Sin.
Eve and Paradise
Reference to Rabbi Yitchak Luria, "Who entered Orchard"

Adam and Original Sin: Reference to Rabbi Yitchak Luria, "Who entered Orchard".

33° Latitude: Location for both Jerusalem the Holy and the New Mexico Territory of New Spain.

Non-Biblical References as Part of Exodus Play

Hermitaño
A dream so profound it landed in this time frame, written as an angel character the Hermitaño

Zacarias
Refers to rebel group from First Jewish War, Sicarrians from the book, the Jewish Wars by Flavius Josephus.

Flavius Josephus writings from the *Antiquities of the Jews*.
Sun took with him
The Sun and the Moon
Sicarrians, Jewish first century Rebel groups in *Jewish Wars* book

Requestado—Relaxed
The Inquisition final punishment, the word relaxed as a soften word for their final act for their prisoner to be turned over to civil authorities for heretic activities in New and Old Spain.

Incline(ing) Human bodies
The writers used this word to show the influence of Greek astrologist Ptolemy in 1258 to reference a location of cosmic study outside of Spain and Judea.
Infinite Pleasure (Delight)
Tree of Life reference from Kabbalists Moshe Cordoviero or Isaac Luria.

Seven Capital Vices
Reference to Coronado de Vasquez false Discovery of the Seven Cities of Gold, la Cibola.

Panel vs Pañel cryptic meaning
Panel refers to swaddling diaper in Portal of Light play.
Pañel is the location of honeycomb cashew apple fruit only grown in the Extremadura region due to the cool climate. Thus, Toledo seems a likely origin of the author's home base.

Semano
The reference to the Ladino Heaven located in the constellation Capricorn.

Tevano-*Chocolate the Drink*
Greek character made reference to the new world delicious "chocolate" drink.

Salla: *I even lost the battle to Salla and Daniel*—**El Diablo**
The word refers to Salla Allah Alai Wassallam, the Islamic Prophet

Muhammad and the joint battle alongside Daniel, a Judaic person against the non-believers in 625 AD. The battle took place in Uhad in northwest area of Rúbal al Khalid desert.

Hermano Penitentes: brotherhood of the Pious Fraternity of Our Father Jesus the Nazarene residing to the regions of northern New Mexico and southern Colorado.

Ladino Hermanos: the cryptic and camouflaged Jewish persons and their families of the brotherhood known as the *Hermandad*.

Appendix B

Themes Comparative Analysis Dead Sea Scrolls and Exodus Play

DEAD SEA SCROLLS

A. Leather Notebooks

Phylacteries
Tefillin **are Sacred Prayers**

Book of Deuteronomy
Wear on arm or forehead

Writers of Scrolls
Qumran Writers

B. Essenes Belief

Yeridah-Markalot
Throne has been Seated in Chariot
Seated Throne refers to Ezekial

Wind: Clouds his chariot, walks upon
Wings of Wind

Creation
Time Frame prior to Year Qne B.C.
Belief in One Creator

Philosophy
Request Messiah Free Oppression
Earth Born Messiah-Essenes
Adult delivered Messiah-Pharasees

Genesis Story "The Fall"

Fallen Angel became Devil, theGenesis Story
Thy Wisdom, No Measure

JORNADO DE EXODO

A. Leather Cuaderno-Notebook

Cuadernos
Tafilla **are Sacred Prayers**

Alabados are Sacred Songs
Hold Cuaderno to heart and lips

Writers of Alabads and Exodus Play
Ladino Hermano Penitentes Writers

B. Essenes Belief
Bible and Torah
Before Light of Day, Appears
Before Golden Chariot
Took Throne from Me, El Diablo
Mount the Winds
Glad you Return from Wind, Tubal

Creation
Born is most beautiful child...
Belief in One Creator

Philosophy
Messiah provide libertad
Earth Born Messiah-Hermanos

Genesis Story "The Fall"

El Diable is protagonist in story
Knowledge without Equal

C. Language
Aramaic, Hebrew, Paleo Hebrew, Greek in Scrolls
Esoteric Knowledge maintained
Use Aramaic language to conceal Cosmic analysis
Use Aramaic Language conceal knowledge
Greek language spoken by populace in year One
Book of Tobit written in Greek
Aramaic-Syriac spoke by Flavius Josephus
Oral Language precursor of Mishnan Language
on Copper Scrolls
D. Essenes with Knowledge of Aramaic Language
Sons of Light
Use of Solar Calendar follow Celestial Equator
Annual Festival days on Calendar never fall on Sabbath
Aramaic Essenes brought knowledge Kabalah to Iberia
Tree of Life broght to Spain
E. Not disclose Esoteric or cosmic knowledge
Zodiac Calendar on Copper Scroll
Esoteric knowledge concealed in Aramaic language
Knowledge flow to Iberia
Sleep is Vision
Dreams used to move story
Seek Pleasure
Tree of Knowledge-Genesis Story originated
Zealots-leadership siezed command Masada prior to invations by Romans

C. Language
Ladino, Spanish, Hebrew used in Play
Use Ladino Language Conceal Cosmic Knowledge
by Hermanos de Luz-Brothers of Light
Use of Ladino Language conceal knowledge
Greek format of Play
Mention of Apollo and Pluto
Alabados intially were passed down as oral psalms
D. Essenes with Knowledge of Aramaic Language
Brothers of Light-Hermanos de Luz
Follow Celestial Equator with Cosmis study
Kaballah brought to New Spain 13th Century
E. Not disclose Esoteric or cosmic knowledge
Knowledge Twin Suns in Universe
Semano is Heaven Capricorn Constellation
Knowledge of Portal of Light
Kabbalah written in Aramaic in Spain
When sleep, Hermitano obtains vision
Dreams used to move story
Infinite Pleasure
Moshe Cordoviero-Tree of Life
PARDES techniques hide story
Sacarias in Exodus play, aka Zealots

Son of God Fragment (4Q246) likely Angel

As Minsters of the Glorious Face are Angels

F. Biblical Characters

Devil (Bileal)
Son of Darkness
Roman Soldiers-Kitta
Venom and Dragon
Depth to...Hell

Michael-Angel (Melchizedek)
Son of Light

Time Traveler
Uriel the Angel
Thou Earth...Deep

Daniel
Sixty-Two Weeks: Coming of Melchizedek-Michael
Dreams
King seated on throne, a vision or dream..

Dreams used to tell story
Dreams requested to seek knowledge

*Leafy Dawn Passage **is the** Portal of Light*
Deep Portal Guarded by Angels
Formula for the Conscious Directive
Time + Direct Matter + Direct Energy = Conscious
F. Biblical Characters
El Diablo
Science of Manipulation
Dark Heart
Roman Catholics and Christians
Venom and Dragon
Depth to abyss..
Michael-Angel
Angel tells of born Messiah
Time Traveler
Hermitano
Deep Portal Guarded by Angels
Daniel
God coming in Sixty Two weeks
Dreams so profound, landed in this time frame, said Hermitano
Light Dreams
Dreams so profound, landed in this time frame
Lost furious battle of Daniel and Salla

Adam: Adam rule over it..
Eve: She (Eve) gave birth
Herod ruled Jewish community
Messiah-Anointed One
Was to Teach the Truth
Healing the wounded and resurrecting the dead
When God engendes the Messiah, he shall come…
G. Biblical Words
Good News to the Poor
Dominion (double meaning)
The Dominion of the Kittiim shall come to end
Redeem the Soul of the Poor
Redeem the Poor
Love
Love God with All Heart
Perdition
In Dark Places of Perdition
Knowledge without Equal
Roots of Wisdom
Born of truth
Swadling Clothes
Sorrowful: Abraham, I was Sorrowful
Light is with him..
Ezekiel's Passage
Happy is a man that is (happy) given
The Dark Light
Invaders-Persecutors

Adam permitted eat forbidden tree..
First Mother Eve
Rely on Herod for evil acts
Messiah
Messiah to be born
He is the Promised Messiah
Angel apprears to Hermitano: Messiah coming
G. Biblical Words
Good News
Destroy forces of my Dominion
Redeemer of the World
Redeem the Poor
Love
Love of Life and Heart
Perdition
Man's heart is Perdition
Knowledge without Equal
Roots of Mountain
Born on Straw
Swadling Clothes
Remedy for out sorrows
Light that appears..
Leafy dawn Passage
Infinite happiness
The Dark Light
Persecutors

Romans-Kimmit (defined as Group in Power)
Punishment
Death, torture, slavery, flogging, outcast
Those in Charge
Roman Legion
Generals of Battle
Soldiers of Battalions
The Light
Michael Arch Angel
Rafael Angel
Hymns
Uriel Angel
Used **to tell Noah** *End the Flesh*
Uriel used to travel cosmos
Named
Essenes: Judah
Essenes called themselves: The Community
Zealot's siezed command Masada prior invasion by Romans
Chariot Image as type of Kabbalist
Merkavah=Vision of Chariot
His throne was flaming with fire..
Provide Image Image/Sign God motivate
Chariot is Sign God motivate Jew Warriors to fight Romans
Chariot seated in cloud
One God-*Yaway*
Merkavah **imagery is central of Book of Daniel**

Spanish Catholics and Christians
Punishmen
Death, torture, flogging, outcast
Those in Charge
Office of Inquisition-Spain
Archdiocise of Durango, Mexico
Priests and those operate Quemaduras
The Light
Angel apprears to Hermitano: Messiah coming
Rafael as angel battles El Diable
Michael Arch Angel
Hemitano is time traveler
Emmanuel is Light
Exodus Play used to share of Light
Alabados-Hymns conduit share light
Named
*Serenitas **affectionately by those who know community***
*Maranos **or Swine by Spanish Catholics***
*Sephardic-Sefardim **from Universal Communities***
*Sacarias **in Exodus play, aka Zealots***
Chariot Image as type of Kabbalist
Before Light of Day, Appear Golden Chariot
*surrounded by fire...eternal hell-**El Diablo***
*took throne from me--**El Diablo***

Ascent	
those who enter to the chariot ascend and are not harmed	
ascend [to the seventh palace] and are not harmed...	
H. Concealment	
Ability to Hide Historic Text in Caves	
Hid Scrolls in Jars in Caves	
Fortold repression by Romans, hid before Temple sacked	
Scrolls hid to preserve for Judaic history to survive	
Knowledge of Essenes and Law Moses	
Faith of Law of Moses	
Spirituality belonging to Essenes preserved	
Cosmos shared via Zodiac Calendar in Copper Scrolls	
Conceal knowledge of Nazarine within Essenes	
Conceal arrival of Anointed One in Age Aquarius	
Testing of Faith	
Essenes placed in Situation for God Testing Fath	
Scrolls to be Discovered at Later date	
33 Degree Insight	
Mosada Caves exist at 33° latitude	
The Light	
Essenes are Sons of Light	

Ascent
Before Light of Day, appear (at night) the Golden Chariot
*why taking journey?--**Bacto***
enter Chariot....there is no equal in all the
so profound, landed in this Time Frame
H. Concealment
Ability to Hide Historical Text in Christian Play
Hid Text in Cryptice Text of Cuaderno
Hid play in early development of laws and rituals of Hermano Penitentes
over 100 years prior to Edict of Fe-Edicto de Fe announced in churches
Conceal Ladino language and Dual meanings for survival
Historical knowledge of Essenes and Scrolls preserved
Faith of Law of Moses
Spirituality belonging to Essenes preserved
Cosmos shared in Portal of Light, Semano and Conscious Directive
Preserve Sephardic history as their faith survives
Share arrival of Anointed One in Age Aquarius
Testing of Faith
Ladinos placed in Dual Faith Situation for God Testing Fath
Exodus play to be Discovered at Later date
33 Degree Insight
Sephardic Jews sought live at 33° of Jeruselum
the Holy in new Spain
The Light
Manhatton Project
Ladino's lived and worked on Project
Robert Oppenheimer selects Los Alamos site at 33° latitude
Scientists team designated the "luminarias" by Oppenheimer
Laboratory of reseach and experiments faces North-Northwest to watch horizon of Sun

Light Revealed
Beginning of Age of Pisces

Fuller House many windows face South tracting horizon movement of Sun
Light Revealed
Exodus Play released at beginning of Age of Aquarius

Glossary of Words, Phrases and Concepts

Age of Aquarius: The Time Frame and astrology beginning of the 21st century, akin to the end of time noted by Aztec and the Mayan calendar.

Alabados: Songs of Psalms specific to brotherhood Los Hermanos Penitentes, originated and first sang in acapella prayer form in expedition of American southwest by Juan de Oñate in 1598.

Anointed One: The word Mashiach comes from the root Mem-Shin-Chen, which means to paint, smear, or anoint, refers to the ancient practice of anointing kings with oil when they took the throne. Known from the gentile prospective as the New Messiah.

HaMashiac: Hebrew word is the literal translation meaning Messiah, describing a future savior person to come.

Artificial Intelligence: Applied and General artificial intelligence that has established dependency and dominance over human society.

Blue Planet: One of the sacred words used in the Exodus Play of 1733 to describe our Earth.

Believers: Followers of traditional and faith of either Christianity and Judaic faith and Believe in the arrival of the New Messiah Anointed One and the Continuum.

Non-Believers: Those not of genuine faith as Believers.

Anointed One: The *Mashiach*, whose translation is the translation that will used as the *Anointed One*, in this writing to refer to the new Anointed One in the 21st Century.

Book of Enoch: *The ancient* Hebrew apocalyptic religious text, ascribed by tradition to Enoch, the great-grandfather of Noah. The book contains esoteric material regarding origins of Portals, time traveling Angels, and the Great Flood-Deluge, written 200-300 before BC.

Enoch contains unique material on the origins of demons and giants, why some angels fell from heaven (The Fall), an explanation of why the Great Flood was morally necessary.

Christian Messiah: The word Moshiah comes from the root Yod-Shin-Ayin, which means to help or save, this the determinant of the Essenes values as Healers or to Save as in Savior. The Divine or semi-divine being who will sacrifice himself to save us from the consequences of our own sins is a Christian concept.

Cistern: The Essene created tank or pool used for constant daily bathing rituals.

Continuum: accepting of the concept that the existence of Jesus of Nazareth is a Continuum of the Judaic faith.

Copper Scrolls: were Essene in origin and written in Aramaic, preserving the Zodiac Calendar sharing knowledge of Constellation movement and the celestial equator.

Corporate Elite: Corporate Elite share specific recognizable traits of being connected and development of liberal corporate establishment, the Scientific, Intellectual, Engineering, Managerial and Financial elites that control Wall Street.

Essenes: The word Essene mean Community and this group called themselves Judah-*Yahad*. *The brotherhood* flourished during Second Temple era (c. 250 BC– 70 CE) with strongholds in rural regions such as Galilee near the Sea of Galilee. The nonmaterialistic brethren were never mentioned in either the Torah or Bible.

Exodus Play: Play provided cryptic Judaic history shared among Jewish families in New Spain.

Faith of Light and Belief: is NOT based on Skin Color, rather one's belief of the ways of light.

Herkhalot; "the vision of the chariot is not a vision, rather is a Palace or a place."

Flavius Josephus: Jewish rebel, General, converted Roman historian and author, spoke languages of Paleo Hebrew, Hebrew, Greek and studied and lived Essene, Jewish and Roman lifestyles.

Forgiveness: The Jewish community application of the concept of *mechilah*, forgoing of the other's indebtedness to facilitate this process. The Christian community application of forgiveness, this concept taught by the Essene trained Jesus of Nazareth.

Iberia: Considered the one-time joint sovereign countries of both Spain and Portugal.

John the Baptist, the Essene: Healing and prayer were the virtues of an Essene.

Masada fortress: Home of the Essene community and location of the hidden Dead Sea Scrolls, the fort is atop of an isolated rock plateau on eastern edge of Judean Desert overlooking the Dead Sea. Akin to a mesa, 20 km (12 mi) east of Arad.

Ladino: Person of Judaic history from Spain also known as Sephardic or *Sephardim*, may speak Ladino Language.

Ladino **Language**: Hybrid Spanish and Hebrew languages (similar in concept to Yiddish, the blending of German and Hebrew).

Kabbalah: the ancient Jewish tradition of mystical interpretation of the Bible, began with the early Jewish mystics, applied by the Aramaic Essenes and later developed into formal body of studies by Jewish scholars in Spain beginning in the 13th century.

Markalot: The *Yeridah-Markalot* vision of the chariot, the "Throne has been seated in Chariot" and that of the Chariot "Appears,"

New Messiah: The word *Moshiah* comes from the root *Yod-Shin-Ayin*, which means to help or save, this the determinant of the Essenes values as Healers or to Save as in Savior. The Divine or semi-divine being who will sacrifice himself to save us from the consequences of our own sins is a Christian concept. The arrival of the New Messiah as a foretelling of the *Ladino Hermano Penitentes*.

New Spain: Generally considered the American Southwest including parts of Arizona, Colorado, New Mexico, Texas are parts of northern Mexico.

Old Spain: vintage Spain in Europe.

Qumran: Archaeological site in the West Bank, the home and location of fortress of the Essene brotherhood, the site closest to the buried treasure and hidden Dead Sea Scrolls.

***Salbe Luna Hermana*-Save the Sister Moon Alabado:** Jewish influenced Alabado shared in book, Shared Lives, Twin Sun

Semano-Heaven definition from Ladino dictionary

Sefarfin: Individuals that origin of Spain or Portugal expelled to other countries including the New World by monarchy at the end of the 15th Century. Known as Sephardic Jews.

Seranitas: Affectionate term used by Christian community to identify the cryptic Judaic Ladino community in the American Southwest.

Teacher of Righteousness: The Essene explanation, individual had been sent to establish for them a *new Covenant*, which was to be the sole valid form of the eternal alliance between God and Israel. This individual is not disclosed by Essenes or mention in scrolls.

True Israel: The Essenes considered themselves the faith of *True Israel*, their study of the scrolls, non-material life style and belief in the Oneness of nature and spirituality distinguished this fraternity from all other beliefs.

Uriel the Angel: is utilized as a Time Traveler, able to travel to separate realities to link stories of past and present. Uriel as the Time Traveler, visiting different Ages or Time Frames and using Portals to enter these Ages of Time Frames. Uriel shares the cycles of the universe to disclose making of astronomy and horoscopes an original revelation.

Bibliography

Introduction

VERMES, Geza The Complete Dead Sea Scrolls in English, Penguin Books 1962

Garcia, Anthony *The Portal of Light*: Kabbalah, Emmanuel and the Church (Kindle
Locations (571-3573), Jornado de Exódo-Journey of Exodus, 2017

Garcia, Anthony *Shared Lives, Twin Sun*, Jornado de Exódo-Journey of Exodus, 2017

Discovery Chapter

Book of Enoch:
https://www.billkochman.com/Articles-Non-BBB/enoch-06.html

Chapter 1

Josephus, Flavius The Jewish War, 1 BC

UTRUVIAN MAN: LIBRARY OF CONGRESS, Leonardo de Vinci
totallyhistory.com/vitruvian-man/

Yashanet.com The 22 paths and the ten Sephirot form a series of 16 "triads" within the Tree of Life.

Chapter 2

Shearer, Tony *Lord of Dawn, Quetzalcoatl and the Tree of Life* Publication Date: 1971, version 1 Nature Graph Publishers (1995 v. 2)

Shearer, Tony *The Praying Flute: Song of the Earth Mother: A Bald Mountain Story* (Children's Book) published in 1975

Sidnie Crawford, *Where Were the Dead Sea Scrolls* Qumran caves reveal lost scroll secrets Biblicalarchaeology.org, January 4, 2017, January 4, 2017

Chapter 3

Joseph, Simon *Jesus as an Essene* Bibleinterp.arizona.edu, January 2018

Josephus, Flavius *Antiquities of the Jews* January 93 AD Written in Greek Language originally

Garcia, Anthony *The Portal of Light, The Sun Took Sun and Moon*, page 212

Chapter 4

Josephus, Flavius *What Josephus says about Essenes in the Judaic War*

www.orion.nscc.huji
www.orion.mscc.huji.ac.il/orion/programs/Mason00-1.shtml
Lendering, Jona *History of Josephus*, 1997 *www.Livius*.org

Chapter 6

Salla, Michael E *Ruler of Earth*, July 2007
www.Bibliotecapleyades.net

From Enoch to John: http://orion.mscc.huji.ac.il/symposiums/10th/papers/regev.htm

The book of Enoch and Dreams
paganizingfaithofyeshua.freeservers.com/intro_book_enoch.htm

ssenes and Ascension/Heaven: http://www.earlyjewishwritings.com/ascensionisaiah.html

Chapter 7

Leonardo da Vinci, Walter Isaacson, Simon & Schuster, 2017

New Yorker magazine, The Secret Lives of Leonardo da Vinci
newyorker.com/magazine/2017/10/16/

Hawking, Stephen
May be the worst event in human history and it is best to employ best practices to establish boundaries of usage for AI.

Factor-Tech Magazine, Factor-Tech.com   March 14, 2018

Chapter 9

Cordoviero, Moshe (Remak) Pardes Rimonim, *An Orchard of Pamegranates*

Solar Calendar, bibarch.com/concepts/calendrics/essene_calendar.htm

Cryptic Aramaic Teaching earthsky.org/astronomy-essentials/taurus-heres-your-constellation

Tauris in Southern sky: solarsystemquick.com/universe/taurus-constellation.htm

Moon passing through Zodiac Sings, cafeastrology.com/whenthemoonisin.html

Crab Nebula
solarsystemquick.com/universe/taurus-constellation.htm

X-ray: NASA/CXC/SAO; Optical: NASA/STScI; Infrared: NASA-JPL-Caltech

A Walk Through Time article, phys.org/news/2018-03-crab-nebula.html

Bill Gates, "I don't understand why people are not concerned" Dangers of Artificial Intelligence Washington Post, January 9, 2015
washingtonpost.com/news/the-switch/wp/2015/01/28

Chapter 10
Salbe Luna Alabado, *Shared Lives, Twin Sun* Anthony Garcia

Chapter 11
Kai Fu Lee My Journey in AI:

The Story Behind the Man Who Helped Launch 5 AI Companies Shoshana Zuboff The Age of Survellience Capitalish:

The Fight for a Human Future at AI

Pedro Domingos, The Master Algorighm: How the Quest for the Ultimate Learning

VERMES, Geza The Complete Dead Sea Scrolls in English, Penguin Books 1962

Mystical Knowledge among the Essenes, (4Q405 20, ii– 22) Page 77 of 679

Chapter 12
Gilpen, Emilee COVID-19 crisis tells world what Indigenous People have been Saving

Canada's National Observer, March 2020

Chapter 13
Who will be Messiah: www.jewfaq.org/mashiach.htm

Criteria to be Messiah
jewsforjudaism.org/knowledge/articles/messiah-the-criteria/

Revised Standard Version Catholic Edition 54
Isaiah 53:1-4 Description of Jesus

Josephus, Flavius   Antiquities of the Jews, *Crooked Back.*

Phillip R. Davies, Damascus Document, Shared History of Islam and Christianity

Damascus Covenant, JSTOT Press 1983

Exhibits

Vitruvian Man: Library of Congress:
leonardodavinci.net/the-vitruvian-man.jsp   better source
loc.gov/item/00650441

Tree of Life: Study of Book of Revelations
yashanet.com/studies/revstudy/rev6htm

Addendum A
The Future Shared in the Technology of the Portal of Light

Earth Sky Magazine Capricorn - earthsky.org/astronomy-essentials/capricornus-heres-your-constellation

Phys.org A Walk Through Time Crab Nebula
phys.org/news/2018-03-crab-nebula.html

Nasa/JPL Crab Nebular Credit: X-ray: NASA/CXC/SAO; Optical: NASA/STScI; Infrared: NASA-JPL-Caltech

Maestas, Robert   The Portal of Light Graphic Drawing Shared Lives, Twin Sun page 32-33, 2015

www.ingramcontent.com/pod-product-compliance
Lightning Source LLC
Chambersburg PA
CBHW071001160426
43193CB00012B/1863